THE
HISTORY
OF THE
ROMAN WALL

By

W. HUTTON
The First Man to Walk the Wall

REPRINT OF THE 1813 EDITION

This publication has been set in new type but
the old spellings and capitals have been kept

ISBN 085983 1302
This edition 1990

Published by FRANK GRAHAM, NEWCASTLE ON TYNE

Engraved by James Basire

WILLIAM HUTTON ESQ. F.S.A.S. ÆT. 81.

Published by J. Nichols & Son, 1st Nov. 1804.

THE

HISTORY

OF THE

ℜ𝔬𝔪𝔞𝔫 𝔚𝔞𝔩𝔩,

WHICH CROSSES THE ISLAND OF BRITAIN,

FROM THE GERMAN OCEAN

TO THE IRISH SEA.

DESCRIBING

ITS ANTIENT STATE,

AND

ITS APPEARANCE IN THE YEAR 1801.

———

By W. HUTTON, F. A. S. S.

———

THE SECOND EDITION; WITH CORRECTIONS.

═══════

LONDON:

PRINTED BY AND FOR NICHOLS, SON, AND BENTLEY,
RED LION PASSAGE, FLEET-STREET.
SOLD ALSO BY F. JOLLIE, CARLISLE; W. CHARNLEY,
NEWCASTLE; R. DICKENSON, HEXHAM; BEILBY AND CO.
BIRMINGHAM; AND J. DREWRY, DERBY.
1813.

TO JOHN NICHOLS, Esq.

SIR,

I TAKE the liberty, without soliciting your consent, to inscribe this Work to you.

Although your laborious and successful pen has embraced a County; you will not overlook a few mutilated Ditches, and a broken Wall. It is characteristic of the spreading Oak, to shelter the humble Bush.

Whatever is worthy of remark, will attract your eye. – Though your humanity will feel, for the antient animosity, the plunder, and murder, upon the Borders of the two respectable Nations; yet you will rejoice, that concord is established along the line of the Wall; and that, instead of rancour, robbery, burning, and blood, civilization has not only taken place, but even generosity.

You will also pardon the errors of the Work; for you know I was not bred to Letters, but, that the Battledore, at an age not exceeding six, was the last book I used at school.

I am, Sir, respectfully,

Your obedient servant,

WILLIAM HUTTON.

Birmingham,
April 13, 1802.

ADVERTISEMENT TO THE SECOND EDITION

THE kind intentions of my highly-respected Friend Mr. Hutton, in presenting me with this Work, were frustrated by an unfortunate Accident, which consumed all the Copies of it that were then unsold.

Enough, however, were in the hands of the publick, to establish its character, and considerably increase the reputation of its ingenious Author.

The good opinion I originally entertained of the Work, is so strongly confirmed by the unanimous Approbation of the various periodical Critics; that I cannot resist selecting some passages from the principle ones:

"Singular characters undertake singular adventures, and relate them in a singular manner. We have a case in point before us. A gentleman, at the age of 78, takes a pedestrian journey of 600 miles, with a black wallet and an umbrella at his back, to explore the whole length of Severus's Wall, for the purpose of ascertaining its present state! Animated by the enthusiasm of an Antiquary, the relics of this the most stupendous monument of Britain might be to him a matter of curiosity; but can an old man render his account of an old wall interesting? Yes. Mr. Hutton, though by no means in his *second childhood',* is as alert and playful as a kitten; and that reader must be saturnine indeed, who can peruse his book without being amused. We will not say that Nature, after she made Mr. Hutton, 'broke the mould:' but we may venture to assert that we might stand at Charing Cross, and not meet one individual like him. If he has oddities, he has much sense and goodness of heart blended with them; and he seems to have more wit than commonly falls to the share of an Antiquary. From the title of his work we anticipated no great entertainment: but we were agreeably disappointed: and his tour to the Roman Wall has afforded us not less pleasure than information. — This tour, the result of singular enthusiasm in a man of 78, will be of use in correcting the errors of writers who have copied from each other without examination. Mr. Hutton supposes that he is the only man who has travelled the whole length of the wall, and is probably the last who will attempt it. The former part of his assertion may be true: but it is not unlikely that his book may put some other Antiquary on the trot; and if this should be the case, we recommend it to him to take a servant, provided with the means of excavating the earth near the military stations; for it must be remembered that, if Mr. Hutton, considering his age, performed wonders, his survey was rapid, and merely superficial. Any farther examination, also, should be undertaken without much delay; for this Antiquarian Pilgrim states, with great indignation and sorrow, that important dilapidations are making on the remains of this precious relic; and he gives it as his opinion, that it has suffered more in the last century, than in the fifteen preceeding."

Monthly Review, March 1806, *p.* 269.

"Mr. Hutton has often contributed to the entertainment of the publick, and is very facetious and good-humoured. At the age of 78, Mr. Hutton undertook and performed a journey of six hundred miles, to see what he laughingly calls 'a shattered wall', but what really is the first and most remarkable specimen of the Antiquity, which our Island has to boast. Camden, Horsley, Warburton, and Gough, have all treated on the subject; but probably the present Author is the only individual who ever traversed the whole length of the wall. His narrative is accompanied by many pleasant anecdotes, related in his accustomed tone of vivacity and humour; and by eight plates, illustrative of the objects of his journey."

British Critic, Jan. 1803.

"Various circumstances have called off our attention from the works of this lively and respectable Veteran, whose 'sear and yellow leaf' of life is well employed in little excursions, which he describes with peculiar spirit and *naïveté*. The Roman Wall seems to have haunted Mr. Hutton's fancy from his early years. Not the tomb of Amandus and Amanda so filled, of yore, the mind of the facetious, the whimsical Yorick: but more happy our Author; for he found at least the remains of a wall on which to drop a tear, the ruins of another Troy, over which he might heave a sigh. This 'wonderful structure — the united work of a commander in chief and two emperors, assisted by three powerful armies, and aided by a long series of years,' — he at last visited at the age of 78, having walked 600 miles to see a shattered ruin. Mr. Hutton blames, with equal justice and severity, the usual dry forbidding style of the Antiquary. He has pursued a different path. — Our Author's Tour is entertaining in many respects, and in some instructive. We leave him with regret; but we shall soon rejoin him in his way to North Wales, and again accompany him to Scarborough."

Critical Review, 1804, Vol. III. *p.* 187.

"The entertaining, interesting, and novel manner which this worthy Veteran adopts in his topographical and antiquarian writings, must be pleasing to almost every class of readers. In the Preface to the Present work, we discover particular and engaging traits of the Author's mind, and at the same time meet with that information on the subject, and on Antiquities in general, which afford us much gratification. Mr. Hutton proceeds to relate some historical particulars of this celebrated rampart, and discriminates the parts that were erected at different periods, and by different generals. This part of his work furnishes many interesting traits of the history and policy of the Romans, and strikingly characterises the unhappy times when plunder, murder, and all the consequent miseries of savage war, conspired to deluge the plains with blood. — Mr. Hutton gives a description of his journey in tracing the Wall from the first station at Segedunum, or the Wall's end, to the eighteenth station, Tunnocelum, now called Boulness. In this excursion he meets with various characters, scenes, and incidents, which are related with much good-humoured quaintness; and the account he gives of the present appearance of the works serves to gratify our curiosity, and correct some mis-statements of preceding writers. — The preceding extracts and remarks will enable our readers to appreciate the character of the volume before us, which on the whole we consider as·an amusing and interesting portion of topographical history. The lively and cheerful manners of the Author captivate the fancy, and we follow him through the progress of his journey with sympathy and curiosity. The venerable relick which attracted his notice excites the latter; and we cannot but sympathize with the respectable and amiable Author, who at the age of 78, undertook such a 'laborious, romantic, and quixotic undertaking,' as he terms it."

ATKIN'S *Annual Review,* 1802, *p.* 468.

"You never can bring a WALL; — What say you, Bottom?"
"Some man, or other, must present WALL?" SHAKSPEARE.

"We have received much pleasure in reviewing former topographical works of this Writer, who keeps up the ball of curiosity and narrative to the last. Some good stories, and suitable observations on them, are told of the state of the Border, and the debatable ground in succeeding times, till the latter was divided between the two nations in 1549. — At Penrith the father and daughter parted — he for the Wall, she for the lakes. Antiquaries as we are, we wish they had kept together."

"Thus have I, WALL, my part discharged so,
And, being done, thus Wall away doth go." SHAKSPEARE.

Mr. GOUGH, *in Gent. Mag.* 1804, *p.* 633.

Sanctioned by such respectable authority, I hesitate not to submit this second Edition to the candour of the publick.

On application to its venerable Author, who, at full twenty years beyond the age of man, still enjoys his strong mental faculties, I was favoured with some material corrections; accompanied by a letter from his excellent daughter; which I am permitted to prefix to her Father's work, for the gratification of its readers; who will not be displeased to see the Portrait of Mr. HUTTON, introduced as a Frontispiece to the Work.

Oct. 1. 1813.   J. NICHOLS.

"TO JOHN NICHOLS, Esq.

DEAR SIR,	*Bennet's Hill, June 3,* 1813.

My Father is happy to find his 'Roman Wall' possesses such a portion of your esteem as to engage you to re-print it. He has nothing to add on that subject; but I transcribe the copy of a letter of my own, written some years ago to Mr. Pratt, who requested me to furnish him with some particulars of my Father's journey. Though my letter was written without any idea of its being published, Mr. Pratt thought it contained so faithful a picture of my Father, that he asked, and obtained, leave to insert it in his 'Harvest Home.' This, however, for some reason of his own, he declined doing; and it is very much at your service, if you think it a proper appendage to your new edition of the 'Roman Wall.' My Father says, it tells him more of himself than he knew before, and has copied it into his Manuscript Life.

I am, dear Sir, with great regard, Your very grateful and obedient servant,

CATHERINE HUTTON."

"TO S.S. PRATT, Esq.

DEAR SIR,

Our summer's excursion in 1801 was ardently wished for by us both. My Father's object was, to see the Roman Wall; mine, the Lakes of Cumberland and Westmoreland. We talked it over, by our fire-side, every evening the preceding winter. He always insisted upon setting out on foot, and performing as much of the journey as he should be able in the same manner. I made little objection to his plan; reserving myself for a grand attack at last.

When the time drew near, I represented to my Father that it was impossible he should walk the whole way; though I agreed with him that he could walk a considerable part: the only difference between us was, whether he should ride to prevent mischief, or after mischief was done. I besought him, with tears, to go as far as Liverpool in a carriage, and walk afterwards as he might find it expedient; but he was inflexible. All I could obtain was, a promise that he would take care of himself.

I rode on a pillion behind a servant; and our mode of travelling was this. My Father informed himself at a night how he could get out of the house the next morning, before the servants were stirring. He rose at four o'clock, walked to the end of the next stage, breakfasted, and waited for me. I set out at seven; and, when I arrived at the same inn, breakfasted also. When my Father had rested two hours, he set off again. When my horse had fed properly, I followed; passed my Father on the road, arrived before him at the next inn, and bespoke dinner and beds.

My Father was so careful not to be put out of his regular pace, that he would not allow me to walk by his side, either on foot or on horseback; not even through a town. The only time I ever did walk with him was through the street of Warrington; and then, of my own accord, I kept a little behind, that I might not influence his step. He chose that pace which was the least exertion to him, and never varied it. It looked like a saunter; but it was steady, and got over the ground at the rate of full two miles and a half in an hour.

When the horse on which I rode saw my Father before him, he neighed, though at the distance of a quarter of a mile; and the servant had some trouble to hold him in. He once laid the reins upon his neck; and he trotted directly up to my Father, then stopped, and laid his head on his shoulder.

My Father delivered all his money to me before we left home, reserving only a few pieces of loose coin, in case he should want on the road. I paid all bills; and he had nothing to do but walk out of an inn, when he found himself sufficiently refreshed.

My Father was such an enthusiast with regard to the *Wall*, that he turned neither to the right or the left, except to gratify me with a sight of Liverpool. Winander Mere he saw, and Ullswater he saw; because they lay under his feet; but nothing could detain him from his grand object.

When we had reached Penrith, we took a melancholy breakfast, and parted, with a tear half suppressed on my Father's side, and tears not to be suppressed on mine. He continued his way to Carlisle; I turned westward for Keswick. After a few days stay there, I went back to Hest Bank, a small sea-bathing place near Lancaster, where we had appointed to meet.

While I remained at Hest Bank, I received two scraps of paper, torn from my Father's pocket-book; the first date from Carlisle, July 20; in which he told me he was sound in body, shoe, and stocking, and had just risen from a lodging among fleas. The second from Newcastle, July 23, when he informed me "he had been at the Wall's End; that the weather was so hot he was obliged to repose under hedges; and that the country was infested with thieves: but, lest I should be under any apprehensions for his personal safety, he added, they were only such as demolished his idol, the Wall, by stealing the stones of which it was composed."

On the fifth morning after my arrival at Hest Bank, before I was up, I heard Father cry *Hem!* on the stairs. I answered by calling out *Father!* which directed him to my room; and a most joyful meeting ensued. He continued here four days, wondered at and respected by the company. We set out on our return home in the same manner as before, and reached it in safety.

During the whole journey I watched my Father with a jealous eye. The first symptom of fatigue I observed was at Budworth, in Cheshire; after he had lost his way, and been six hours upon his legs; first in deep sands, and then on pavement road. At Liverpool his spirits were good; but I thought his voice rather weaker. At Preston he first said he was tired; but, having walked eleven miles farther, to Garstang, he found himself recovered; and never after, to the best of my remembrance, uttered the least complaint. He usually came into an inn in high spirits, ate a hearty meal, grew sleepy after it, and in two hours was rested. His appearance never forsook him. He regarded strong liquors with abhorrence. Porter he drank, when he could get it; ale and spirits, never. He mixed his wine with water; but considered water, alone, as the most refreshing beverage.

THE AUTHOR'S PREFACE

THERE are few pursuits, in the compass of letters, more dry than that of Antiquity. The Antiquary feeds upon withered husks, which none can relish but himself; nor does he seem to possess the art of dressing up his dried morsel to suit the palate of a reader, for his language is often as dry as his subject; as if the smile was an enemy to Truth. Mere dull description, like a burnt cinder, is dead matter. If he designs a *treat*, why not infuse a little spice to suit the taste of his guest?

The description also of Antiquities is not only the dullest of all descriptions, but is rendered more dull by abstruse terms; by as much Learning as the Author can muster, and Latin, as the page can conveniently hold. Instead of inviting, it rather repels a reader. Thus Truth, dressed out like a beau, in flourishing trappings, is scarcely known; but would please in a plain dress.

My dear and learned Reader, though I treat of the Latins, I have no Latin with which I can treat you. My language, like myself, will display something of the Quaker.

I would enliven truth with the smile, with the anecdote; and, while I travel the long and dreary Wall, would have you travel with me, though by your own fireside; would have you see, and feel, as I do; and make the journey influence your passions, as mine are influenced.

The Antiquary values a piece according to its authenticity. A piece of coin, not worth a shilling, will bring many times its intrinsic worth, when its history is known. But, if its Antiquity be ever so great, if the history be dark, the value is no more than its weight.

When pieces of Antiquity are common, like old clothes, they lose much of their consequence. Thus, the coins found at *Verulam*, which I have seen by handfuls, are almost rated at nought.

If the mind is delighted at the sight of a *watch* worn by Charles the First; a sword carried through France before Edward the Third; a *spur* worn by William the Conqueror; or with a Danish battle-axe; what astonishment must arise at the sight of the grandest production of Art in the whole Island! the united work of a Commander in Chief and two Emperors, assisted by three powerful armies, and aided by a long series of years!

Having had the pleasure of seeing many Antiques of various ages and people, it naturally excited a desire of proceeding in farther research; and the eye, unsatisfied with seeing, induced a wish to see the greatest of all the curiosities left us by the Romans, *The Wall*, the wonderful and united works of Agricola, Hadrian, and Severus.

I consulted all the Authors I could procure; which strengthened desire. But I found they were only echoes to each other. Many had written upon the subject; but I could discover, that very few had even seen it, and not a soul had penetrated from one end to the other. Besides, if those who paid a transient visit chose to *ride*, they could not be minute observers.

Poor CAMDEN travelled it till he was frightened, ran away, and wrote hastily. HORSLEY was weary, and retreated; but wrote more correctly. The judicious WARBURTON, whom I regard for his veracity, rode on, desisted, and then remarked, "He believed he had trod upon ground which no foot had ever trodden since the Romans." He also transcribes HORSLEY, whom Mr. GOUGH professes to follow.

I envied the people in the neighbourhood of the Wall, though I knew they valued it no more than the soil on which it stood. I wished to converse with an intelligent resident, but never saw one.

I determined to spend a month, and fifty guineas, in minutely examining the relicks of this first of wonders; began to form my plan of operations, and wrote my sentiments to an eminent Printer in London, for whom I have a singular regard; but, receiving no answer, I gave up the design, and, as I thought, for ever; destroyed my remarks; closed with regret all my books of intelligence, and never durst open them, lest it should revive a strong inclination, which I could not gratify.

About four years elapsed, when my family agreed with a gentleman and his lady to visit the LAKES. They enlisted me of the party, in which they found no difficulty, because the temptation lay in the neighbourhood of that wonder which had long engaged my ideas.

I have given a short sketch of my approach to this famous Bulwark; have described it as it appears in the present day, and stated my return.

Perhaps, I am the first man that ever travelled the whole length of this Wall, and probably the last that ever will attempt it. Who then will say, he has, like me, travelled it twice?

Old people are much inclined to accuse youth of their follies; but on this head silence will become me, lest I should be asked, "What can exceed the folly of that man, at seventy-eight, walked six hundred miles to see a shattered Wall!"

W.H.

Birmingham, April 13, 1802.

BOOKS BY THE SAME AUTHOR.

1. The History of Birmingham, 8vo. 9s.
2. The Journey to London, 12mo. 2s. 6d.
3. The Court of Requests, 8vo. 7s.
4. History of the Hundred Court, being a Supplement to the Court of Requests, 1s.
*5. The History of Blackpool, frequented for Sea-bathing, 8vo. 2s. 6d.
6. The Battle of Bosworth Field, 8vo. 7s; or with a Continuation by Mr. Nichols, illustrated with Plates, 12s.
*7. The History of Derby, 8vo. 7s. 6d.
*8. The Barbers, a Poem, 8vo. 1s.

*9. Edgar and Elfrida, a Poem, 8vo. 1s.
10. Remarks upon North Wales in sixteen Tours, 8vo. 7s. 6d.
*11. Poems, chiefly Tales, 8vo. 10s. 6d.
*12. Tour to Scarborough, 8vo. 7s.
13. Trip to Coatham, 8vo. 10s. 6d.

The Miser Married, a Novel.
BY CATHERINE HUTTON.
3 vols. 12mo. 15s.

* Those Books with an Asterisk, are out of print.

THE HISTORY OF THE ROMAN WALL, &c.

THIS first, and most remarkable piece of Antiquity in the whole Island, is known by several names, some of them erroneous. It bore that of *Agricola*, which is now lost. *The Picts Wall;* but this seems inconsistent, for they had no concern with the Wall, except to pull it down; and I think it should rather bear the name of man who built it up. Sometimes *Hadrian's Wall;* but I cannot see why a bank of earth should bear the name of *a Wall*. Our idea of a wall comprehends an erection of brick or stone. Perhaps Hadrian's *Bank* would be more in character, as agreeing with the materials of which it is composed. *Severus's Wall* is more proper, because he erected the stone wall, part of which is remaining. It is often called *The Roman Wall*, and, by way of pre-eminence, *The Wall*.

That *man* is born a savage, there needs no other proof than Severus's Wall. It characterizes two nations as robbers, and murderers. Nineteen in twenty of our race sustain half this character during life. Some individuals correct the crude passions, adhere to justice, and avoid whatever is worthy of blame.

The first intentional act of a child is an attempt to scratch the eyes of its mother; the next, wilfully to disobey orders; another, to gripe a young cat round the neck, and enjoy with a smile the agonies of death; a fourth, forcibly to take the play-things from a boy less than himself, and, should the loser complain, toss his hat into the street, and kick his posteriors. To punish the brute creation opens a wide field for ferocity; as impaling insects, winging butterflies, and, if possessed of a whip, never to let a dog pass without using the lash.

The next step, as he rises into years, is to hunt after property not his own, which he tries to acquire by deceit, chicane, finesse, and, if he cannot accomplish it, would take a pleasure in destroying it, that another may not possess it. Should pride, or influence, prompt him to act fairly, only increase the temptation, and you find the rogue Thus nineteen in twenty declare war against the creation.

This Wall is also a clear proof, that every species of cruelty that one man can practise to another was here, and pronounces the human being as much a savage as the brute. This place has been the scene of more plunder and murder than any part of the Island, of equal extent. During four hundred years, while the Wall continued a barrier, this was the grand theatre of war, as well as during ages after its destruction.

Some learned and worthy men, pryers into human nature, have contended, "that civilization increases, and that the world is advancing towards perfection." – Light, and knowledge, I allow, have made an amazing progress during the last ages; but that is owing to commerce, and the printing press. This, however, comes under the word *polished* society, not *honest*. Man may be better informed, but not mended; or why did the Spaniards, and Portuguese, in latter ages, butcher the natives in South America by millions, and take their property? And why did we, though in a small degree, follow their example in the North?

Perhaps a Scotsman would consider this mighty bulwark a compliment paid to his country; and infer, "it was designed to bar a superior power, and was the effect of fear; for, if two nations could meet upon equal terms, there would be no need to raise a wall between them."

A Roman would reply, "Your country is mountainous, barren, and difficult to conquer. The rough *land* is your safeguard, not the people; and the inhabitants are so poor, they are not worth conquering. On these rests your security." There may be, in both these remarks, a wider opening for truth than for boasting.

Our old historians always term the Scots *Barbarians:* to this I assent. They surprized the innocent, murdered them, laid waste their country, took the property, and *left the place*. Allow me, without the aid of Dr. Johnson, to illustrate the word *Barbarian*. Julius Caesar, Agricola, Antonine, Severus, &c. went one step farther than the Scots; they surprised, murdered, plundered, and *kept possession*. Our venerable ancestors too, the Saxons, Danes, and Normans, who came over in swarms, butchered, robbed, and possessed; although they had no more right than I have to your coat. Whoever deprives an unoffending man of his right, comes under this word. It follows, no war can be justified but that of defence.

It is an old remark, that "idleness is introductive of mischief." The *Picts*, now Highlanders, confirm this remark. Strangers to commerce, to the arts, and, from the barrenness of the country, almost to agriculture, they led a life of indolence. Their chief avocations were hunting, basking in the sun, procuring fuel from the heath, and fish from the water. In some of these, the women bore a part.

Idleness of body promotes idleness of mind. They were savage voracious, domineering, except to their chiefs, who were as savage as themselves, but to them they paid implicit obedience. Servility is the attendant upon a mind debased.

Men thus situated must feel the effects of want. Nature and necessity made them courageous. At the beck of the chief, they entered the Lowlands, which they sometimes robbed; but oftener joined the inhabitants in partnership, and penetrated the borders between Scotland and England; and, when not opposed, killed, burnt, and pilfered, at pleasure; then returned, singing in Erse, their native tongue.

While the Britons were supine, or quarelling with each other; or while their power was withdrawn from the frontiers, and employed against other enemies; the Scots and Picts made their inroads. Booty was the word; but this could not be had without blood.

This astonishing rampart, the production of three eminent persons, and at three different periods, was designed to remedy the mischiefs described.

AGRICOLA's WORK

WHEN Agricola, the ablest general, and most accomplished statesman of the age, commanded the Romans in Britain, he led them into Scotland, in the year eighty-four, to punish the depredations of the natives. He found *Galgacus*, their general, with an army of thirty thousand men, encamped upon the Grampian hills, ready to receive him. He gave them battle, defeated them, and drove them back into the Highlands.

Being master of the country, and willing to prevent such evils as had occurred for ages, he erected what our historians call a *Wall*, as a bar against the Picts. This was principally a bank and a ditch; on the borders of which he built, at unequal distances, a range of castles. This work extends from sea to sea, about seventy-four miles, beginning three miles and a half East of Newcastle, and ending twelve West of Carlisle, which, while guarded, curbed the enemy: the spot suited, as being the narrowest part of the Island.

HADRIAN's WALL, OR RATHER WORKS

AFTER Agricola's works had continued about thirty-seven years, often injured, as a bank of earth easily might, by an enemy constantly upon the watch; the Emperor Hadrian, in the year one hundred and twenty-one, repaired the works of Agricola, and added some of his own to strengthen them. These were, joining to Agricola's small ditch, which lay towards the North, a large one, making a large rampart, and then finishing, as Agricola began, with a small ditch; all their works running in parallel lines.

From this time Agricola's lost its name, and the whole to this day has absurdly retained that of *Hadrian's Wall*. So that what now bears his name, as the work of one man, was really the work of two.

SEVERUS's WALL

THE Northern adventures were quiet while the works were new, and a regular defence continued. But, military attention diminishing, the desire of the Picts increased.

Hunger is said to "break through *stone* walls:" then what security in walls of earth! It is difficult to keep out an enemy, who is determined not to be kept out. Inroads were quickly made, and former tragedies acted. No newspapers to convey the tidings of the day, no post to reveal distant transactions, nor commodious roads to convey either: the unfortunate residents were off their guard; and, had they been on, they could not have warded off the blow. The first intelligence of an approaching enemy appeared to the eye, instead of the ear, and he brought destruction in his hand.

Upon unprosperous adventures, the Picts sued for peace, always obtained it, and, to keep them quiet, upon easy terms.

When the unhappy Britons had fluctuated between life and death, eighty-seven years after Hadrian's work was completed, Severus was chosen Emperor. Two years were spent in reducing his enemies on the continent, after which he came into Britain.

Penetrating into Scotland, the enemy fled where Severus durst not follow; and the Picts exulted, it is said, that their unwholesome water, their keen air, their bogs, meres, mountains, impenetrable woods, and slender sustenance, but particularly the incessant labour of Severus's men, had destroyed fifty thousand without a battle. Many skirmishes, however, were fought, chiefly in favour of the Romans. The Picts solicited peace, which was granted upon condition that they should lay down their arms and retire.

Severus, at rest, considered, that as many a fine army might be destroyed in reducing a people not worth reducing, he had better confine them within their own boundary. To accomplish this, he determined, in the year two hundred, to repair the works of the two former chiefs, injured by time, but more by the enemy, and erect a wall of stone, guarded by a ditch which should run parallel with theirs, and make one grand and compact work. Thus every contrivance of man is set up against the knavery of man. And now the inhabitants of the borders rejoiced in the prospect of security: instead of being plundered by their enemies, they would be protected by their friends, who had full power to protect.

It may seem surprizing, that by the erection of these works, the Romans must have relinquished to the enemy a vast tract of country, extending eighty miles North, and in breadth, from the German ocean to the Irish sea, about ninety, the best land in Scotland. The human capacity is nearly the same in all ages; whatever reasons we can find for the conduct of the Romans, we may be assured they could find for themselves. – They began to be apprehensive they should weaken the state by extending dominion, a thought which ought to strike us. And Severus considered, that building the Wall was an arduous task; that this was the only place where he could shorten the work, the shorter the stronger, and the less force would guard it; besides, if the enemy were allowed the above fertile lands, favourable for agriculture, it would lessen the temptation to plunder. *Graham's Dyke* too, or rather the work of Antoninus, between the Frith of Forth and the Clyde, was by long neglect far gone in decay.

Another reason which induced him to fix here was, its affinity to Hadrian's work, which would strengthen his own; and he well knew, the united efforts of human wisdom would be needful to guard against inclination and hunger.

There was no fear of the Romans being molested in their operations, for two reasons: they were masters of the country to the Frith and Clyde, the above space of eighty miles, and the force employed at the Wall was an ample security.

Some authors have seriously disputed, "at which end of the Wall Severus began." But this point will clear itself when we consider that two Legions were employed, the Second, and the Sixth, consisting of about twelve thousand men. A plan of the Wall was first determined upon, divided into four parts; the Second Legion was appointed to the first and third parts, beginning in the East; and the Sixth Legion, to the second and fourth. This is proved by a variety of inscriptions. Perhaps every mile, in this long range, was begun at the same time. This was necessary, because the whole isthmus would be secured, from one sea to the other.

In all laborious undertakings, the Britons were pressed into the service, and charged with the drudgery. In this case, however, where life and property were at stake, there was no need of compulsion.

The Wall was about eight feet thick, and twelve high, to the battlements, which rose about four more; so that, viewed in profile, it would appear much like a chair, the main part forming the seat, and the embattled part the back. At the foot of the Wall, on the North, a ditch ran parallel, the dimensions of which and the wall I shall give hereafter.

STATIONS

ALONG the line of the Wall, the Emperor constructed, of stone, three kinds of fortification, which were *Stations, Castles,* and *Turrets.* The Stations, or Cities, are said to have been eighteen in number, with seventeen intervals, ranged at unequal distances, the average about four miles each. These were fortified inclosures, about one hundred and thirty-six yards square, the Wall itself constituting the North side. They were designed for residence, as well as guard, and were appropriated to the same use as our modern barracks; also buildings for family use, suitable to various occupations.

If the cohorts were full, six hundred and sixty-six military men were probably the lot of each Station. – From this grand body of reserve, were supplied the

CASTLES,

OF which there were eighty-one, called by the country people *Mile Castles,* because they were nearly a mile asunder, or rather seven furlongs. About four of these, on the average, were fixed between every Station. They were about ninety-six feet square, the Wall still forming the North side. The Stations supplied the castles with a guard of perhaps one hundred men each. Every Station commanded, on each side of it, about two castles.

As the Stations furnished a guard for the castles, *they* supplied one for the

TURRETS,

WHICH were small *Castles, Castelets,* or *Watch Towers,* ranged along the Wall, at the distance of about three hundred and eight yards each; consequently there must have been about three hundred and thirty. They were twelve feet square: each castle commanded about ten turrets, five on a side, which were daily supplied with a guard, probably, of two or four men each.

These Turrets being near together, the sound of the voice, trumpet, or shell, would penetrate the whole length of the Wall, if attention was paid, in a short time, when danger approached. This must have been the completest construction, for the purpose, ever invented by human wisdom. And the expence of the watch, enormous.

What length of time these united and immortal works would cost in finishing, is impossible to tell; all our authors are silent; but it could not be so little as thirty years, nor could they be completed for so small a sum as one hundred millions of our present money, exclusive of the land they occupy, which is more than five square miles, or than three thousand acres.

As Agricola's name was lost in Hadrian's, so Severus, being superior to both, nearly eclipses both, and the whole is frequently called Severus's Wall.

Thus we have carried the reader from the beginning to the completion of one of the grandest works of human labour, performed by the greatest nation upon earth. What shall we say of that production, which was the utmost extent of Roman effort, and which stands unrivalled in Europe! How much delight would it afford the modern antiquarian eye, could he survey the works of Agricola, Hadrian, and Severus, as they then appeared! the noblest sight ever beheld in this Island! the work of strength, of genius, and of years! Men have been deified for trifles compared to this admirable structure; a Wall seventy miles in length, furnished with eighteen Cities, eighty-one Castles, and three hundred and thirty Turrets, with all their mounds, roads, ramparts, and astonishing apparatus! One sight would raise the mind to a rapturous sublimity. Man would be lost in the wonder, nor satisfied with a single view. We have admired a wall which has secured only a private mansion; still more, when it surrounded a City; but what ideas can we fix to one which guarded a kingdom!

What I have described is only part of that superb production which crosses the Island; for the three personages, but chiefly Severus, formed various roads, which extended both to the North and South, exclusive of those which ran parallel with the Wall, and which led to various fortified Castles, ten or fifteen miles distant; so that the whole country was a series of fortifications.

These out castles were probably possessed by the Roman officers, to whom, and their heirs, Severus bequeathed the adjacent lands in perpetuity, in consideration of their keeping a certain number of men in arms to guard the frontiers; and which they could not dispose of, except by the same military tenure. This is thought to have been the first instance of the feudal system. – The mighty work obliged the Picts, for a time, to starve at home.

So large a number of people assembled, as the Roman soldiery, with the multitude of Britons drawn to their assistance, together with those who brought materials and necessaries for building, and family use, accounts for the vast number of villages and dwellings which have been near the Wall.

The work of Severus, untouched by the wicked fingers of man, would exhibit its proud head many thousand years; but the works of Agricola and Hadrian, being native earth, would continue to the last trump.

The Wall was now complete, well guarded, and the people safe. But the Roman power beginning to decline, and the military abating in their attention, the Picts and Scots found means to break through, surprized, and slaughtered the Romans, killed their generals, and retreated.

Constantine (not the Great), who reigned towards the close of the fourth century, first neglected the Wall. He collected the flower of the British youth; passed with his army into France; and left this country in a defenceless state. Thus, being exhausted of its strength, the Wall was again broken, and the enemy, with destruction, entered: the people lost their energy, and nothing was seen but desolation.

Theodosius began his reign in 402, and continued near half a century. In his time the Romans withdrew from Britain. The Picts and Scots made inroads; and the inhabitants, in distress, applied to the Romans for assistance, inviting those conquerors, whom they formerly tried to repel. A legion was sent, who beat back their enemies; but, the Roman empire being in convulsions, they were ordered back, and returned no more, after a residence of four hundred and eighty-eight years from the landing of Caesar.

Before their departure, they instructed the miserable natives in the use of arms, the arts of government, of war, and directed them how to repair the Wall. But a most dastardly spirit, such as is rarely found in history, pervaded the whole kingdom. They were more inclined to weep over their situation, than attempt to improve it. Let not a people vaunt; what they *have* been, they *may* be. The sovereign was weak; the people were slaves.

In this dreadful state of existence, without energy, the Wall went to decay, after that noble monument had remained in perfection two hundred years, and was never after effectually repaired.

Gildas, who lived near this period, remarks, "As soon as the Romans were departed, hideous multitudes of Scots and Picts came swarming out of their *Carroghes*, like whole armies of black vermin, at high noon, crawling out of their narrow holes; which, though they differed in other things, agreed in bloodshed. They seized the Northern parts, as if they had been their own inheritance, even as far as the Wall;" (which proves that the Lowlands were the property of the Romans.)

"Against these attempts, there were ranged, in the high parts, along the Wall, garrisons of soldiers; but such as were both slothful, and unserviceable for martial affairs; which white-livered lozels, with quaking hearts, *sat still* watching day and night, till their joints were benumbed, and were as stupid as the stones on which they sat, so that their unarmed enemies, with long hooks, plucked the miserable watchers off the Wall, and dashed them against the ground till dead. Thus by their sudden deaths they escaped those calamities which awaited their families, relations, and friends; for they abandoned the Wall, their abode, and departed wherever they could hide themselves. But the enemy pursued with violence, slaughtered, massacred, and rent them to pieces like lambs in the hands of bloody butchers, or in the jaws of savage beasts."

In these dreadful times, the distressed were obliged to rob each other to support life; this brought on numberless quarrels, which, as the land denied relief, continued a length of time. Their chief support was hunting and fishing.

During the following five hundred and fifty years, while the Saxons held the rule, a continual warfare was sustained on the borders, between the two kingdoms; sometimes by armies, but more frequently by small parties of the neighbouring inhabitants. The land near the Wall was often the property of a Scotch sovereign, and often that of an English monarch; but so full of thieves and murderers, it was not worth owning by either; and yet, though the two Princes could agree upon many points, they could not agree upon a line of demarcation. The people lived without restraint, and without protection.

It is impossible to conceive a human being in a more dreadful situation than that of a borderer; keeping, in the day-time, a continual look-out, and in the dark and solitary night, attentive to every minute sound, which excited terrible ideas, and augmented those ideas into the approach of an enemy. His property ever open to plunder; his house, the only thing immovable, exposed to the flames; his mind perpetually tortured by the rack, surrounded by enemies, all bred up in savage principles, wishing to take his life, and he who could take it, might with impunity; his only guard was his strength, which, put into the balance against a multitude, was a dram to a pound. His wife and children, the dearest treasures upon earth, daily liable to be murdered before his eyes, and himself doomed to share their fate or starve! Bread, water, and peace, is preferable to such a life, even with an entail of ten thousand acres.

Some idea may be formed of the ruined state of the country; for, at the general Domesday survey of the kingdom in 1080, the four counties of Cumberland, Northumberland, Durham, and Westmoreland, were omitted; because, by the continued wars between the two nations, they were so ruined, and covered with marks of destruction, that they must have been surveyed with horror, but without profit.

Three of these counties, Northumberland, Cumberland, and Westmoreland, were, at the Conquest, in the hands of the Scots; but they soon lost them, for William gave Cumberland to his favourite, and follower, *Randolph Meschines*, who parcelled out the dangerous frontiers among his officers upon the feudal system. To some he gave a Knight's fee, six hundred and forty acres, of the annual rent of twenty pounds, to some, half one; and to others, a quarter; furnishing them with men and arms, to guard against invasion, keeping the centre himself, part of which was the forest of Inglewood.

Randolph, like a true patriot, would not suffer the military to be idle; for, being at peace, he distributed his men over the country, which is fertile, to cultivate the land. He gave the Barony of Burgh to Robert Treavers, which descended by marriage to the Morvilles. The head of this family was Sir Hugh Morville, one of the four Knights, who, in 1169, murdered Thomas Becket, Archbishop of Canterbury; which as soon as they had accomplished, they entered the bishop's stables, took four of his horses, and, travelling private ways, hid themselves at Knaresburgh, in Yorkshire, the property of Hugh.

It does not appear that these four gentlemen set out from Normandy with a resolution to kill Becket. Many charges, arguments, and expostulations, passed between them during some time, in which, had the Bishop been in the least complying, the evil had been voided; but, the Knights irritated for the moment by his stubborn replies, destruction to the man ensued, who merited every punishment but the last.

This Sir Hugh was also proprietor of Kirk Oswald, near Penrith. He erected the church in expiation of the crime, where his sword, in memory of the transaction, was preserved for many ages. *Danton* says, that the sword which killed Becket was, in his father's life-time, (Queen Elizabeth) kept at Isel, the property of Hugh, and afterwards in the Duke of Norfolk's family, who are descended from Hugh.

The Barony of Burgh came afterwards by marriage to the Moltons, then to the Dacres, and the Howards Dukes of Norfolk, who married the heiress of Dacre.

The military, in time of danger, were collected by firing the beacons; and were, by the laws of tenure, bound to serve forty days. The privates enjoyed small farms of ten or twelve acres, called *Nag* and *Foot* tenements. These beacons were erected in the following places in 1468:

Carlisle,	Boot-Hill,
Lingy-Close head,	Mulcaster-Fell,

Beacon-Hill,	St. Bees-Head,
Penrith,	Workington-Head,
Dale-Roughton,	Moothey,
Brampton-Moat,	Skiddow,
Spade-Adam-Top,	Sandale-Top,
Black-Comb,	all in Cumberland.

Stanemore-Top,	Win-Fell,
Farlton-Knot,	Orton-Scar,
Hard-Knot,	in Westmoreland.

The lawless banditti in the borders were on the watch for plunder; and whatever depredations were committed in one kingdom, were never punished in the other; so that, if the offender could either fight or fly, he was safe.

Exclusive of the want of a general line of demarcation, there was a piece of common land, about ten miles long, and six broad, called *Debatable Ground*, claimed and possessed by both, about five miles North of the Wall, joining Solway Frith; this harboured the greatest number of thieves, because the title of either crown was defective. Thus property, instead of being protected by the law, could only be protected by strength, and this was not with the owner. Society cannot exist without a compact; besides bred among savages, he became savage himself.

An old Roll describes the boundary of the Debatable Ground as follows: "Beginning where Stark meets the sea, then up to Pyngilburn, then to Pyngilburn-Know; thence to Righeads, then to Monk-Riland-burn, and down Harven-burn to the Esk; to the foot of Terras; up Terras to the foot of Reygill; up Reygill to the top-house; then to the standing stone, and the Mereburn-head; then down till it falls into the Lyddall at Rutterford; and still down till it falls into the Esk; and thence into the sea."

Which side formed this Roll of division is uncertain; but the description is so very intelligent, that a stranger might find it. The circumference was perhaps thirty-five miles. Had equity decided upon the Debatable Ground instead of arms, she would have given it to Scotland.

This degraded piece of land, this scene of butchery, gave rise to that celebrated joke upon "King James's favourite *Cow*, which he brought from Scotland when he acceded to the crown. She having no taste for English manners, silently retreated without even a farewell to the monarch; and was the only personage in his whole train that ever returned to Scotland. When the courtiers expressed their surprize, how she could find the way, as she could speak neither Scotch nor English; the King replied, *that* did not excite his wonder so much as how she could travel over the Debatable Ground without being stolen."

The loss of the three counties sat uneasy upon the mind of the Scotish sovereigns, who did not chuse to assert their right during the martial spirit of the Norman kings; but when the affairs of Kind John were embroiled with the Pope and the Barons, William, King of Scotland, demanded them; when John, distressed for money, ceded them, with some other privileges, to William, in 1209, for fifteen thousand marks, equal to about two hundred thousand pounds of our present currency; but the money was never paid.

Alexander, the son of William, demanded them afterwards of Henry the Third, the son of John, or that he should fulfil his father's contract; but Henry was too poor, or too dishonest, to do either. Bargains between princes are kept, while it is their interest.

After many applications, the two Kings met in 1237 at York; and agreed, that Alexander should resign his pretensions to the three counties for a yearly pension of eight hundred marks, and two hundred librates of land; and that Henry's brother Richard, King of the Romans, should marry the King of Scot's sister.

As this agreement also was not performed, the two sovereigns met a second time at York, and fabricated a third, which, I have reason to think, was observed just as well as the others.

After Edward the First had reduced Scotland, he resided some time in Cumberland; and hearing daily complaints of the mischiefs committed on the borders by the banditti, appointed Robert de Clifford Lord Warden of the Marches, as they were afterwards called. The lords of manors were placed under his command, and bound to serve, with a stipulated number of men, horse and foot, armed, and supported at their own expence. A revival of the feudal tenure.

The Lords Wardens had almost an unlimited power: they could hold courts, take cognizance of offences, punish the body, could fine, seize lands, or goods, could upon the appearance of an enemy call into actual service all able-bodied men from sixteen to sixty, lead them into action, and make truce, or peace, with the Scots.

This office continued during many reigns. In Queen Elizabeth's time, the salary of the Lord Warden was four hundred a year, out of which he paid two deputies.

The Lord de Clifford continued in office till slain at the battle of Bannock Burn in 1314, where the English are said to have lost fifty thousand men, which so depopulated the country, that few men were left. An order was therefore issued, "that no man should sleep more than two nights with one woman, but proceed from house to house, and reinstate the lost generation." Perhaps this was the first order of the kind ever made; an order which would probably be kept.

From this time, the Kings of Scotland claimed an equal right with those of England to appoint Lords of the Marches. In this, Richard the Second acquiesced because he could not help it.

Percy, Earl of Northumberland, was constituted for England, and Douglas, Lord Galway, for Scotland. A jury was established; the English lord chose six out of Scotland, and the Scotch six out of England. The defendant, upon the trials, was acquitted upon his own oath. Surely they knew but little of human nature, or they would have doubted whether one half of those oaths were true when taken by an *interested* man. As the oaths are singular, I will transcribe them.

Juror's Oath

YOU shall clean no bills worthy to be fouled: you shall foul no bills worthy to be cleaned; but shall do that which appeareth with truth, for the maintenance of truth, and suppressing of attempts – So help you GOD.

Plaintiff's Oath

YOU shall leile (little) price make, and truth say, what your goods were worth at the time of their taking, to have been bought and sold in the market, taken all at one time, and that you know no other recovery but this – So help you GOD.

Defendant's Oath

YOU shall swear by Heaven above you, Hell beneath you, by your part in Paradise, by all that GOD made in six days and seven nights, and by GOD himself, you are whart and sackless, of art, part, way, witting, ridd, kenning, having, or reciting, of any of the goods and chattels named in this bill – So help you GOD.

We may observe a mildness in the plaintiff's oath, and severity in the defendant's as well as something foolishly wanton. There appears also no reason why *one* should be accepted, and the *other* disregarded.

Notwithstanding the power of the Lords Warden, on both sides of the Wall, their juries, and courts of justice, yet incursions were made by both kingdoms, as the watchful eye of villany could find an opening. Many battles were fought, and many prisoners taken, as well by fraud as fighting, and charged with a ransom according to their rank, which was the perquisite of the taker.

The Wall was broken through near Stanwix, and the Scots attacked Carlisle; but the fair sex defended the place by a new art of war, scalding the enemy with floods of boiling water from the battlements. Nor were the English secure, had the Wall been perfectly guarded; for the Scots, in parties, frequently boated over Solway Frith, by night, two miles wide, a little West of the Wall, plundered the inhabitants, and retreated before morning.

At the battle of Solway Moss, near the Wall, in the reign of Henry the Eighth, 1543, the English with one thousand men, *are said* to have beaten the Scots with fifteen thousand; but this was a victory without honour on one side, or disgrace on the other; for we are told, that Oliver Sinclair, the Scotch King's favourite, but hated by the people, proud of office, was carried upon men's shoulders, to shew himself and his commission as general. The troops were so disgusted, they refused to fight, but grounded their arms, and suffered themselves to be taken; a preconcerted plan, no doubt; or the English, with their small number, durst not have attacked.

Henry possessed an extension of mind, both for good and evil actions, equal to his extension of body. At Christmas, in the same year, he invited to dinner, at Greenwich, twenty-one of the Scots nobility and gentry taken at this battle, whom he liberated without ransom; perhaps in gratitude for the above plan. Some of their names are as follows:

Prisoners.	By whom taken.
Earl of Cassil,	Batill Routledge took the man, and claimed half the horse, and John Musgrave the other half.

Earl of Glencarn,	Willye Grame, called Watt's Willye, Willye Grame of the Balie, Sir Thomas Wharton, and Thomas Dacre.
Lord Fleming, the King's Privy Counsellor,	George Pott and Stephen James.
Lord Maxwell, Admiral of Scotland, Lord Warden of the Marches, and Privy Counsellor,	Edward Aglionby and George Foster.
Lord Summerville,	Richard Briscoe.
Lord Olivant,	Thomas Denton, James Allison.
Lord Gray,	Thomas Whyte, Willye Storey, and George Storey.
Oliver Sinclair, General and Privy Counsellor,	Willye Bell.

The Lord Warden is said to have summoned to this battle, in his department, the following Lords of Manors, with the force they were obliged to send by their military tenures to protect the frontiers.

Gentlemen.	**Manors.**
John Musgrave, horse and foot,	Beaucastle.
Thomas Blenerhasset, 60 horse.	Gilsland.
Richard Warwick, and tenants.	Warwickbrigs.
Alex. Apleby, 2 horse.	
William Porter, 2 horse.	
Anthony Highmore, 4 horse.	
Edward Aglionby, horse and foot.	Ainstable.
Rob. Briscoe, horse and foot.	
Cuthbert Hutton, 6 horse, 10 foot.	Penrith.
Tho. Dacre, horse and foot.	Graystock.
William Pickering, 20 horse, 20 foot.	Barton, Martindale, and Patterdale.
Chris. Threlkeld, 4 horse, 6 foot.	Threlkeld.
Lancelot Lowther, horse and foot.	Derwentwater Estates.
Mr. Lotus, 60 horse.	Lord Millum.
John Senhouse, 4 horse.	Calder.
William Pennington, all horse.	Mulcaster.
Sir James Lowther, 100 horse, 40 foot.	Whitehaven, &c.
Sir Thomas Curwen, horse and foot.	Workington.
John Lamplugh, 10 horse, 4 foot.	Lamplugh.
Thomas Dykes, 4 horse.	Wardel-Hall.
Richard Eaglesfield, 6 horse.	
Anthony Barwise, 2 horse.	
William Asmotherby, 2 horse.	
John Swimburn, household servants.	
Lord of St. Bees, 10 horse.	
Robert Lamplugh, household servants.	
Robert Ellis, 2 horse.	
John Thwaits, household servants.	
John Shelton, 4 horse.	Basinthwait, and
Sir William Musgrave, 100 horse, 40 foot.	Lowswater.

John Leigh, 10 horse.
Thomas Salkeld, 4 horse.   White Hall.
William Shelton, 6 horse.
Thomas Dalston, 10 horse, 20 foot.   Dalston.
William Vaux, 4 horse, 6 foot.   Catterland.
Richard Blencow, 6 horse.   Blencow.
Bishop's tenants, (Carlisle), 40 horse.
Abbey Holm, all tried horse.

The above military list was in part destroyed, which occasioned some of the gentlemen, and more of the manors, to be omitted; but the total number of men were 1027, another indication of a prior plan of surrender, for we cannot suppose *one* thousand men would attack *fifteen*.

We may observe, that the dignified clergy, notwithstanding their peaceable profession, were obliged to contribute their quota; that the force was chiefly horse; that many of the families still possess the same property, without being goaded with an arbitrary martial tax; and, that those who sent their servants, would be apt to retain a smaller number, and perhaps with bodily defects, that they might slip the shoulder from under the burden.

The *Debatable Ground,* as remarked, had always been an object of dispute between the two crowns. Each kingdom depastured upon this vast common. The Scots were clamorous, or silent, according to the power of the English sovereign. Lord Dacre, who commanded the Western march, informed the Duke of Somerset, Protector, in the reign of Edward the Sixth, 1549, "That the Scots were raising forces, which were to join those of France, and make a descent, with ten thousand men, to burn and destroy whatever was found upon the Debatable Land; and that the numerous and plundering family of *Grame* (Graham), a sturdy race, would turn Scots, if not supported."

An agreement, however, prevented the sword from being drawn: two gentlemen from each kingdom were deputed to settle the boundary; Lord Warton and Sir Thomas Challoner, for England; Sir James Douglas and Sir Richard Maitland, for Scotland. In all disputes, the fewer the number employed to compose them, the sooner the work will be accomplished. They divided it by rivers; but where there were none to guide them, then by a bank and ditch, which they effected from the river Esk, to the Sark, called *The Scotch Dyke,* about five miles long. The North was allotted to the Scots, and the South to the English, which last is now the estate of Sir James Graham, of Netherby, upwards of ten thousand a year. Three hundred and ninety acres of this land, were, in 1771, destroyed by the overflowing of Solway Moss, now re-instated.

Although this division of the land made peace between the two crowns, it did not between the borders. Their depredations continued till the union of the two kingdoms in 1706.

The following is a list, delivered to the Bishop of Carlisle, of the principal offenders, with their followers, who made incursions into Cumberland, and Westmoreland, and were present at the murders, burnings, &c.

Simon Musgrave, Lord of Pattinsor,
Jock Kinmont, Will's Arthur,
Richie Grame of Bailie, Will's
Jock Grame,
Rich. Grame of Askesha-Hill,
Adam Grame of Hall, Richie of Bushe,
Forgie's Wille Grame,
Geordie's Christie,
Black Jock's Johnie,
George Grame of Sandhills,
Dick's Davie's Davie,
Geordie Armstrong of Catgill,
Hector of Harelowe,
Emie of Gingles, Mickle Wille Grame,
Richie's Geordie, Geordie of the
Gingles, or Henharrow,
John Nelson, *Curate* of Beaucastle,
Black Jock's Johnie,
Black Jock's Leonie,
Will's Jock, Richie Grame, jun.
Netherby,
Sandie's Rynyon's Davie,
Gibb's Davie's Francie,

Jock of the Lakes, Christie,
John Noble, alias Longfoot,
Will Grame of Rosetrees,

Will Grame, brother to Hutchin.
John Musgrave, Catherton,
Gibb's Jock's Johnnie, Tom's Robbie,

Pattie's Geordie's Johnnie,
Young John of Woodhead,

Rich. Grame, son of Goodman of Barken Hill,
John of the Side, (Gleed John)
Young Lord of Graitney,
(the famous Gretna Green)
Archie of Gingles, Jock of Gingles,
Watt Grame, (Nimble Wattie,)

Will Grame, (Mickle Willie,)
William Patrick,
Priest of Beaucastle, Red Rowey Forster,
&c.

In this list, we find some names in elevated life, but not of elevated manners. As they were not governed by laws, it was so fashionable to be rogues, that it annihilated disgrace. We see also, among them, the Clergy; who, instead of persuading others from robbery, ought to have been hanged themselves for being robbers.

It was ordained by the commissioners of the border-laws of England, that a council should be established in every March, to be convened twice a year, to try the notorious robbers, who, if found guilty, should suffer death; or, if fugitives, their houses should be destroyed.

On the Scots side of the *Wall,* William Douglas, in 1468, convened the borderers in council; when it was ordained, "That no person shall have any concern with an English man or woman, under pain of high treason, without special licence. If any man steals, the goods shall be taken from him, and he be deemed guilty of treason."

I shall state some of the charges brought by the West Marches of England, to the commissioners, against the Marches of Liddesdale, in Scotland, taken from Mr. Bell's notes, who, in the reign of Queen Elizabeth, was a member of the Border court, and which probably fell under his eye.

Commissioners.

John Foster, John Selbie,
Richard Lowther, Carmegell.

Alex. Hume of Hutton,
George Young

1580 Nov. Sir Simon Musgrave complains against the Lord of Mangartou; the Lords Jock, Sims Thom, and their accomplices, for burning his barn, wheat, rye, oates, and pease, 1000*l.*

1581. Sir Simon Musgrave, Thom of the Todill, and his neighbours, complain against Robin Ellot of the Park, Sim Ellot, Clemie Corser, Gowen's Jock, and others, for stealing sixty kine and oxen, a horse, and taking Thomie Routledge prisoner.

James Foster of Symwhaite complains against William Ellot of Redhaugh, Adam of the Shaws, Archie of the Hill, and John Ellot of Hawhouse, for fifty kine and oxen, and all his insight (household goods).

1582. Matthew Taylor, and the poor widow of Martin Taylor, complain against the old Lord of Whitaugh, young Lord of Whitaugh, Sims Thom, and Jock Copshaw, for one hundred and forty kine and oxen, one hundred sheep, two goats, and all his insight, value 200*l.* sterling. The murder of Martin Taylor, John Dodson, John Skelloe, and Matthew Blackburn.

1582. Thomas Musgrave, Deputy of Beaucastle, and his tenants, complain against Walter Scot, Lord of Buckluth (ancestor to the Duke of Buccleugh) and his accomplices, for two hundred kine, and three hundred sheep and goats.

Andrew Taylor complains against Robin Ellot, Will his brother, George Simpson, and their accomplices, for sixty kine and oxen, one hundred sheep, and all his insight, 60*l.*

1586. Thomas Musgrave, Deputy Warden of Beaucastle, against the Lords Jock, Dick of Dryup, and accomplices, for four hundred kine and oxen, taken in open forrie from the Drysick, in Beaucastle.

1587. Andrew Rootledge, of the Nuke, complains against Lords Jock, Dick of Dryup, Lancy of Whirgills, and their accomplies, for fifty kine and oxen, burning his house, corn, and insight, 100*l.* sterling.

Clemie Taylor complains against Archie Ellot, Gilbie Ellot, and others, for fifty kine and oxen, all his insight, 100 marks sterling.

The poor widow and inhabitants of Temmon complain against the Lord of Mongarton, for the murder of John Tweddal, Willie Tweddal, and Davie Bell; the taking, and carrying away, John Thirlway, Edward Thirlway, John Bell of Clowsgill, Davy Bell, Philip Twedall, Rowe Carrock, Thomas Allison, George Laycock, and Archie Armstrong; randoming them as prisoners, and taking one hundred kine and oxen, spoil of houses, writings, money, and insight, 400*l.* sterling.

Liddesdale against the West Marches. Bills in the hands of Lord Scroop, found by the Commissioners at Berwick.

Lord of Mangarton complains against Cuddie Taylor, and others, for two hundred kine and oxen, insight 20*l.* sterling.

Lord of Mangarton complains against Mr. Humphry Musgrave, Captain Pikeman, and his soldiers, for taking him prisoner; oxen, kine, horses, mares, sheep, goats, and insight, 1500*l.* sterling.

Lord of Mangarton complains against Adam's Jammie Foster, Matthew Taylor, Sealbie's Hutchin, and Geordie's Hetherton, for two hundred kine and oxen, eight hundred sheep and goats, six horses and mares, from Tunden.

Thom Armstrong of Tinnis Burn, complains against Ensign Knap, James's Adam Rootledge, John Taylor, Geordie Hetherton, and Mark's Tom's Geordie.

Lancie of Whitaugh, complains against Sim Taylor, John Taylor, Cuddie Taylor, for insight, silver coined and uncoined 4000*l.* sterling.

Sim Armstrong of Whitaugh, complains against John Taylor, Adam's Jemie, for eight hundred sheep.

Robin Ellot of Redhaugh, complains against Thomas Carlton, for sixty kine and oxen, four hundred sheep, insight, from the Steile, 200*l.*

Hob Ellot of Ransgill, complains against Thomas Carlton, and Richie of the Moat, for sixty kine and oxen, six horses, three prisoners, 400 marks.

Branche Burnhead complains against Mr. Humphry Musgrave, and Thomas Carlton, for twenty kine and oxen, forty horses, from the Ellots of Burnhead.

John Ellot of the Haugh-house, and Gawen of Rarsgill, complain against Captain Cawell, and his band, with the Clans of Leven, for two hundred kine and oxen, thirty horses.

Names of the persons complained of, which the Lord Scroop had to deliver to the court.

John Taylor,	Sim Taylor,
Mr. Humphry Musgrave,	Pattie's Cuddie, Adam's Jemie,
Geordie Hetherton,	Thomas Carlton,
Geordie, son to Mark's Thomie	Richie of the Moat.

Bills found by the Marches of England, against the West Marches of Scotland.

Commissioners.

John Foster, John Selbie,	Alex. Hume, of Hutton,
Richard Louther Carmigell,	George Young.

1582. Thomas Rootledge, of Todholes, and neighbours, complain against Kymont Jock, Eckie Studholme, Jock of the Calf-hill, and accomplices, for forty kine and oxen, twenty sheep and goats, one horse, insight, 300*l.* sterling.

Dick's Rowie Rootledge, complains against Kymond Jock, Jock of Calf-hills, and accomplices, for thirty kine and oxen, one horse, insight, and spoil, 60*l.* sterling.

James Rootledge, and neighbours, complain against Geordie Armstrong of Calf's-hill, and Jock his brother, with accomplices, for one hundred kine and oxen.

1586. Christopher Burstholme of Breekenhill, against John Armstrong, son of

Sandie, Echie's Richie, Willie Grame, called Will with the Silk, for sixty kine and oxen, one bull, one horse, insight, 200 marks.

Geordie Taylor, of the Bone Riddings, complains against Will Bell, Red-cloak, Watt Bell, Richie Bell, with accomplices, for thirty kine and oxen, insight, 100*l.* sterling.

Walter Grame, William Grame, and tenants of Esk, against William Bell, Red-cloak, Watty Bell, and the Sur-name of Carlisle, for burning their mills, houses, corn, insight, 400*l.* sterling.

William Grame of Steddalls, against William Bell, Red-cloak, Tom Bell, and their accomplices, for thirty kine and oxen, sixty sheep, three horses, insight, 100*l.* sterling.

James Grame, and Hutchin Grame, of Pare-tree, against Will Bell, Red-cloak, Tom Bell and accomplices, for sixty-kine and oxen, one hundred sheep, and insight of their houses, 100*l.* sterling.

Cuddy Taylor, and neighbours, of Hellethirst, against young Christopher Armstrong of Awging-hill, Jock of Calf-hill, Eckies Richie, and Willie Cary (Gatewarden), for sixty kine and oxen, four horses, armour, and insight, 200*l.*

Rowey Foster, John Brinie, and neighbours, complain against Richie Maxwell, of Cavans, and the soldiers of Langholm, for two hundred kine and oxen, two hundred sheep and goats.

The poor widow of Watt's Davie Forgie, against John Hollas, Willie Cany, Eckie's Richie, and Co. for the murder of her husband, forty kine and oxen, two horses, insight, 100*l.* sterling.

1587. James Taylor, of the Cross-rig, complains against Jock of Calf-hill, Kynmont Jock, and accomplices, for thirty kine and oxen, two nags, forty goats, 100*l.* sterling.

Thomas Musgrave, Deputy of Beaucastle, and tenants, complain against Geordie of Calf-hill, Pattie of the Hairlowe, Willie Cony, Eckie Richie, and others, for two hundred kine and oxen.

Thomas Grame, called Watt's Davie's Thome, complains against Eckie's Richie, of Stubholme, Willie Cany, John of the Hollows, with their accomplices, for thirty kine and oxen, two horses, insight, 100*l.* sterling; and taking William, and Pattie Grame, prisoners.

Subscribed by the Commissioners abovenamed.

Would a Mahometan suppose I was treating of Christians! Should a Divine enquire, what improvement Christianity had made in the human mind, he must not go near the Wall.

As we are not to suppose the Scots were the sole aggressors, it is necessary to examine the English side of the Wall: justice demands it.

Bills of damage presented to the English Commissioners done by the English, against the West Marches of Scotland.

Walter Scot of Bransholme, and the tenants of Elrick-house, complain against Will Grame, of Rose-trees, Hutchin's Richie of the Bailie, with their accomplices, for eighty kine and oxen, forty nott, sixteen sheep, one horse.

John Wood, of the Revels, and tenants to the Lord of Cookpool, complain against Richie Grame of the Moat, Forgie's Christie, Richie of the Bailie, with their accomplices, for forty nott, one hundred and sixty sheep, and one horse.

Alexander Kirkpatrick complains against Tom's Geordie Grame, and accomplices, for eighty kine and oxen, six horses, and sixty stotts.

The tenants of Smallhame, against Braid Jock's Jamie, and Forgie of Meadup, for two hundred sheep, two hundred kine and oxen, twenty-four horses, insight, 300*l.*

The Lord of Cowhill, James Maxwell, of Poltrack, and others, of the Water of Naith, against Walter Grame, Davie Grame, Will Grame, brother to Walter, Robert of the Fold, and Richie's Will, for burning Cowhill, Poltrack, Dinhawe, one hundred kine and oxen, five hundred sheep, two hundred horses, and prisoners randomed, 30,000*l.* Scots.

The Lord of Maxwell and his tenants, of Dunhaw, Querelwood, Cowhill, and other places, against Walter Grame, of Netherby, Rob of the Fold, alias Willie's Johnie, Dick's Will, for burning eight hundred onsets (3000*l.* Scots), one hundred kine and oxen, three hundred horses, three thousand sheep, prisoners ransomed, 500*l.* sterling.

Robert Maxwell of Castle-milk, and tenants, complain against Walter Grame of Netherby, Rob Grame of the Fold, and company, for burning house, and corn, 4000 marks, one hundred and twenty kine and oxen, one hundred and eighty sheep, insight, 500 marks.

The tenants of Adam of Carlisle, and the Bells, against Walter Grame of Netherby, Davie, and Wattie his brothers, Richie's Will, Rob of the Fold, for burning Goddesbrig, three thousand kine and oxen, four thousand sheep and goats, five hundred horses, 40,000*l.* Scots.

Sir Robert Maxwell of Dunwoodie, against Walter Grame, Davie and Willie his brothers, Rob of the Fold, Richie's Will, and others, for burning Tinwell, Rawshaw, and Mickel-wood side, six hundred kine and oxen, sixty horses, insight, 10,000*l.* Scots.

James Douglas of Drumlanrig, against Walter Grame of the Fold, and Will his brother, for burning the Laithes at Rose, 20,000 marks, Cumrew, 2000 marks, twenty kine and oxen, forty horses, and five hundred sheep.

Executors of the Lord Johnston complain against Hutchin's Andrew, Hutchin's

Richie, Will of the Rose-trees, Francis of the Moat, and others, for burning Low-ood, 5000*l*. Scots, six hundred kine and oxen, eighty horses, five hundred sheep and goats.

The Earl of Morton, and Herbert Cavans, against Grame of the Fold, Walter Grame of Netherby, George Grame, son of little Tom, and others, for burning Langholm, four hundred kine and oxen, one thousand sheep, two hundred horses, 4000*l*. Scots.

The Warden of Scotland, complains against Walter Grame, Richie of the Moat, and others, for bigging houses, and depasturing cattle, in Scotland; sowing corn to the value of forty chalders, during ten years past, estimating the hard corn at thirty shillings a bow, Scots, pasturing two thousand of nott, and horse, at thirty shillings a head, Scots, two hundred sheep, at three pence a head.

Signed
John Foster, John Selbie, Richard Lowther,
Carmigell, Alexander Hume of Hutton, George Young.

The mind is shocked, it even shudders, at the dreadful murders, robberies, and burnings, in the above catalogue; which is only a small part of the devastations practised in the vicinity of the Wall. This farther proves, that we are savages by nature, and should continue to do so, if not improved by precept, or restrained or protected by the laws of society. I am sorry our own times have exhibited the same ferocity as that found near the Wall; and yet the people in that day, as well as this, would have been angry, had they not been denominated Christians; though I do not recollect, that CHRIST ever dealt in blood, or taught it his followers.

The line of destruction extended twenty miles or more, on each side of the Wall.

After the establishment of the marches, the country was laid under contribution, to pay for watch and ward upon the Wall. As a specimen, *Daham*, in the parish of Dacre, paid seventeen and fourpence, to Kendal Castle, for the support of this guard; a large sum in that day. Others paid in proportion.

The roads and avenues were protected by castles, to prevent the inroads of the marauders; and Penrith castle had a subterraneous passage three hundred and seven yards long, which communicated with the kitchen of Dockwray-hall, in that town; thus, as the besieged could not be battered out, they would not be starved out.

In these dreadful times, whole villages fell a sacrifice, and that often in the winter nights, as more congenial to the black purpose; and the inhabitants were obliged to run, even from food, fire, and clothing, into the cold air, and subsist upon the river, and the field. Had there been no other argument for a union between the two kingdoms, the blood which cried from the borders was sufficient. Much has been said, both for and against it; but one short remark will decide the question.— If the members of a vast family are obliged to reside together, whether is it better to live upon equality, and in harmony, promoting each other's interest, or, each to do the other all the mischief in their power? It may be said, "the Scots lost their sovereignty." They did, just as a little tradesman loses *his*, who, having persued business upon his own account, with small gains, enters into partnership with a greater, and multiplies his accumulations tenfold.

Many of the names in the above list are well known in modern history. Some have since graced the Senate and the Church; and some are an honour to the place in which they reside. Johnny Armstrong, with his eight-score men, whose famous old song delighted me seventy years ago, was probably a member of the house above mentioned.

The use of the sur-name seems to have been but in infancy. The *Ap's* in the Welsh rise from son to father, but here we descend from father to son; thus Black Jock's Johnie, and Jock of the lake's Christie, father and son. Dick's Davie's Davie, father, son, and grandson.

Whether the sufferers were reimbursed is doubtful. It is easier to complain, than find redress. Depredations, however, continue; for, in 1593, the Lord Warden Scroop stated to the gentlemen of the Western Marches the dreadful enormities that were committed, and requested their advice. Their opinion was, "that the Lord Warden had power, and ought to summon the heads of houses before him, and oblige them to answer for themselves, and their dependants."

The first of these was *Goodman Grame* of Netherby, who answered for himself, three sons, six brothers, and fourteen followers.

John Grame, for self, two sons, four brothers, and five tenants.

Fargus Grame, for self, sons, and tenants. The numerous family of Grame was terrible.

This agreement, which consisted only in words, was no more binding than a cobweb. The plunderers had two requisites for mischief, inclination and power. They could fight or run. The *name* of *Goodman,* head of the clan, did not altogether coincide with the character.

The Grames returned to their former course, till James the First became sovereign of both kingdoms; when, in the first of his reign, he issued a proclamation against them, and seized many of the clan, who confessed they were unfit for civilized society.

Many of this mischievous race were in 1606, transported into Ireland, and their possessions given to others.

It is difficult to fasten a rogue, except by a halter. Most of them returned the next year, were sent back, but returned even a second, and a third time, following the same diabolical course till 1614, when James again proclaimed, "That he had, in the first of his reign, issued his proclamation against these violent disturbers of the peace, the *Grames,* who had returned, and committed the same enormities; and that if they were caught in the middle shires, after fourteen days, they should be proceeded against, and capitally punished for their former crimes."

The Lord of Marches, and the Commissioners, declared also, that none of the inhabitants (except the Gentry) in Tindale, Riddlesdale, Beaucastle, Willgavy, the North of Gillsland, Esk-dale, Ewsdale, and Annerdale, should keep any arms, or horse, mare, &c. worth more than fifty shillings sterling, or thirty pounds Scots.

Notwithstanding these prohibitions, the banditti continued to infest the Western Marches, under the name of *Moss Troopers,* who being able-bodied men could fight, and expert runners could elude the watch. Many schemes for their extirpation were devised, but none produced a cure, although the *blood-hound* was introduced, whose powers of body and sagacious nostrils had some effect.

In 1616, a commission was sent to Sir Willfrid Lawson, and Sir William Hutton, stating, that horrid disorders daily increased in the borders, and that slough-dogs (blood-hounds) should be provided, according to the king's proclamation, under the direction of Sir William Hutton, and that he should appoint the watches, where they should be kept, and when used, with a power to punish for neglect of duty.

The dogs were kept at the charge of the inhabitants, and stationed as follows:

One dog above the foot of Sark.
One at the moat, within-side Sark, of Richmond-Clugh.
One at the Bailie-head, for the parish of Arthured, Richmont-Clugh, Bailiff, and Blackwater.
One at Tinker-hill, for Newcastle parish, Bailie, and Blackquarter.
One for the parish of Stopleton.
One in the parish of Irthington.
One at Lanercost, and Walton.
One at Kirklington, Scaleby, Houghton, and Richardby; and
One for Westlington, Rawcliff, Etherby, Stainton, Stanwix, and Cargo, to be kept at Rawcliff.

Villainy, notwithstanding every effort, was loth to quit its old habitations. "It was enacted, in 1662, that as lewd, disorderly, lawless thieves, and robbers, commonly called *Moss Troopers*, infested the borders, residing in large wastes, heaths, and mosses, who through secret ways escaped from one kingdom to another to elude punishment, the justices in sessions should have power to assess the inhabitants of the adjoining counties, to constitute a guard against the injury, violence, spoil, and rapine of the Moss Troopers. Northumberland should be charged with five hundred pounds a year, to support thirty men; and Cumberland with two hundred, for twelve men."

The only cure, however, was that applied in 1706, the union of the two kingdoms; for, though the sovereign was one, the people and the jurisprudence were not. And, whatever objections may be made to this union, experience has proved, that nothing ever happened so advantageous to both.

From this happy period hostilities gradually subsided; and that generation, bred to rapine, dying away, posterity became humanized, the laws of protection and civil life assumed an energy, and property was secure on both sides of the Wall.

Thus we have wandered through the long series of fifteen hundred years; have seen the rise, meridian, and fall, of the grandest work ever produced by European hands; have observed, with a melancholy eye, the depraved state of human nature, the defection of law, of the power to protect, and the instability of property; but, with a smile, have seen the termination of a quarrel, which had continued fifty generations. This short inference may be drawn from the whole: that protection on one side, and liberty and obedience on the other, are the foundations of all just government.

The lively impression, however, of former scenes, did not wear out with the practice; for the children of this day upon the English border keep up the remembrance by a common play, called *Scotch and English,* or, *The Raid* (inroad).

The boys of the village choose two captains out of their body. Each nominates, alternately, one out of the little tribe. They then divide into two parties, strip, and deposit their clothes, called *wad* (from weed) in two heaps, each upon their own ground, which is divided by a stone, as a boundary between the two kingdoms. Each then invades the other's territories; the English crying, "here's a leap into thy hand, dry-bellied Scot." He who can, plunders the other side. If one is caught in the enemies' jurisdiction, he becomes a prisoner, and cannot be released except by his own party. Thus one side will sometimes take all the men and property of the other.

None but the most degraded in manners and character will ever upbraid another for his country.— As the place of his birth is not an act of choice, it cannot be a mark of disgrace.

HAVING described the antient state of the Wall, and manners of the inhabitants, I shall now take the liberty of giving my introductory approach to this once grand object, and describe its present state.

Thirteen months elapsed after we had resolved upon our jounrey, when our friends declined the adventure; but we, having fed upon the imaginary but delightful repast, could not relinquish it.

I procured for myself the exclusive privilege of *walking;* which, of all the modes of travelling, I prefer. My daughter rode behind her servant; and we agreed not to impede each other on the way, but meet at certain inns, for refreshment and rest.

I was dressed in black, a kind of religious travelling warrant, but divested of assuming airs; and had a budget of the same colour and materials, much like a dragoon's cartridge-box, or post-man's letter pouch, in which were deposited the maps of Cumberland, Northumberland, and the Wall, with its appendages; all three taken out of Gough's edition of the Britannia; also Warburton's map of the Wall, with my own remarks, &c.

To this little pocket I fastened with a strap, an umbrella in a green case, for I was not likely to have a six weeks' tour without wet, and slung it over that shoulder which was the least tired.— And now, July the 4th, 1801, we began our march.

SUTTON

AT the end of eight miles, we arrived here, situated upon an eminence, pleasant and healthful. It is said, "Ireland is free from venomous animals," this is free from dirt. The town is neat, consists of two streets, or rather one, and the limb of another, forming a figure resembling the letter Y, and is about one hundred and fifty yards long. It is silent as night; except, as being a thoroughfare between Birmingham and the North, the inhabitants are entertained with the thunder of horses' feet, and the rumbling of carriages.

I was once asked by a grocer of this place, "If I could recommend him to a *good* wife?" — "It is totally out of my way: I had the fortune to procure a good one for myself, whom I value highly; but have never *traded* in so precarious an article. But cannot you accommodate yourself at home?" He replied, "There is not one woman in Sutton that will suit me:" — whether the remark redounds to the honour of the fair sex, I leave to them.

LICHFIELD

IS eight miles more; low, flat, and compact, consisting of fourteen short and dull streets, besides one that is long and lively, owing to its being the great road from London to Ireland, and the West of Scotland. Perhaps there are nine hundred houses.

The cathedral is large, and grand; and, as a national building, is a credit; but considered as a place of divine worship, there is more of ostentation than of use; for the devotional part is small, compared to the remainder. The internal walls are in some places covered with green mould. Perhaps our pious ancestors thought their prayers would rise with double effect from stone fret work and gilt timber. Simplicity is characteristic of Christianity. We have reason to conclude, that the church of the Apostles was a private room, not worth ten shillings a year.

I have been struck with an historical incident which occurred in the boisterous reign of Charles the First. The Close, in which the cathedral stands, was a garrison for the King. Lord Brook, by order of parliament, besieged it; and while surveying the works, through the peep-hole in the side wall of a porch, belonging to a small house in Dam-street, his face was observed by a dumb gentleman upon the battlements of the great steeple, whose name was Dyott, of a respectable family now in the neighbourhood; he levelled his piece, and, though I believe the distance is more than one hundred yards, shop him in the face and killed him. Mine has been at the hole, but (thank Heaven!) in peaceable times.

The porch is removed; but its dimensions are exactly marked upon the pavement. My late worthy friend Mr. Greene, proprietor of an admirable cabinet of curiosities, caused an inscription to be placed upon the wall, when he was chief magistrate, to perpetuate the event.

RUDGLEY,

SEVEN miles, is low and level; has about four hundred houses, and consists of one street, extending about three quarters of a mile, which, like a pack-thread string, is length without width.

STONE,

FIFTEEN miles, a thorough-fare also of one street, like the former, and nearly as long, but better built, and about the same number of houses. The accommodations are good, and the people civil.

A person of my appearance, and style of travelling, is so seldom seen upon the high road, that the crowds I met in my whole journey viewed me with an eye of wonder and inquiry, as if ready to cry out "In the name of the Father, &c. What ar't!" and I have reason to believe, not a soul met me without a turn of the head, to survey the rear as well as the front.

NEWCASTLE UNDER LINE,

NINE miles, is elevated, compact, well built, has ten streets, and one thousand and fifty houses; is smoak-dried by the surrounding works. The Marquis of Stafford's interest sends two members into the House of Commons, from whence their *own* sometimes sends them into that of the Lords.

HULME'S CHAPEL,

SIXTEEN miles, a pretty smart church, inclosed in a smart square of about seven houses. The village consists of about twice that number, in a situation delightful.

WARRINGTON,

EIGHTEEN miles, a crowded place, without room for a crowd to exert itself. It consists of fourteen streets, chiefly narrow; about two thousand three hundred houses, and ten thousand five hundred persons. Their shops are so closely squeezed together, as scarcely to admit a customer.

The most spacious street, but the worst built, is Old Warrington, the end of which joins the present town. This street was, about three hundred years ago, the whole of the place, to which the traveller was ferried over the river Mersey. But, Henry the Seventh expressing a wish to visit his mother, the Countess of Richmond, who had married the Earl of Derby, and resided at Latham, to facilitate the King's passage over the river, the Earl is said to have erected this bridge. Hence the present Warrington took its rise. The visit must have been long in agitation, for one year could not complete the work.

PRESCOT,

NINE miles, seems to have risen from an antient and obscure village to a modern, handsome, and pleasant market-town, from its vicinity to Liverpool. It contains seven hundred and thirty-six houses; and 3,465 inhabitants.

LIVERPOOL,

A PLACE of wonder! It is an old remark, "That a spirited, active, and commercial people, who have seen the world, "are more civilized and humane than "those of recluse life." When my daughter and servant had nearly arrived at Liverpool, they were caught in a shower, and obliged to dismount; one took shelter under a scaffold; the other, under a tree. The lady of the mansion invited man, woman, and horse, under cover, treated all three with the greatest hospitality, and, what was preferable, with a smile.

We had been recommended to the King's Arms in Water-street; but, though we could not be admitted, the master sent his servant to procure us an abode.

The hill, as I descended to the town, abounded with windmills; but the houses, afterwards, rising round them, I observed, had obliged them to shorten sail. The stranger is surprized to see the *street* crowded with shipping! The stile of business is amazing, and is enough to ruin Bristol, and eclipse London.

The sea seems about a mile over. The churches are beautiful, the buildings grand, the Exchange a superb work. Here are 580 streets, lanes, and courts, 11,784 houses, and 77,653 persons, exclusive of sailors, about 4000. There arrived from the 24th of June 1800, to the 24th of June 1801, 5060 ships, which unloaded 489,719 tons, and which paid dock dues 28,365l. 8s. 2d. Hence we infer a rich *Corporation*.

I went on board a vessel of 500 tons, 110 feet long, which was allowed to carry 365 slaves.

It is easy to discover, by the buildings and the streets, the old from the new part of the town.

Among the curiosities I saw, was the famous Dr. Solomon, whom I knew, many years ago, in very different circumstances. We should be apt to conclude, *that* man must sell a large quantity of *health*, who accumulates sixty thousand pounds by the sale, as it is said the Doctor has done.

ORMSKIRK,

THIRTEEN miles, consist of two streets, or four, if you please, for they cross at right angles, six hundred and fourteen houses, and 2554 inhabitants. The town is elevated and pleasant, the people agreeable, and the country delightful.

PRESTON,

TWENTY miles, a large, compact, and populous place, and one of the handsomest I ever saw, is in an elevated situation, and flourishing state, contains 2,231 houses and 11,887 inhabitants. The market is thronged. I believe I saw at least 500 carts, which brought supplies. The marketplace is beautiful. The inhabitants are said to be proud, which I did not observe, except in one person, dressed like a clergyman, who refused a civil answer to the trifling inquiries of a stranger. I was pleased with Lord Derby's house, an elegant building, with the conveniencies of a large town, and the prospects of a charming country.

GARSTANG,

ELEVEN miles, has four streets, or rather one, for the other three do not deserve the name; has sixty-eight houses, thirteen of which are public, and seven hundred and thirty-one souls.

Our arrival was on the evening of the Fair-day, Saturday, July 11, 1801, which becoming rainy, we were amused from the windows with the country lasses, large as troopers, in their best array, with their garments tucked up to avoid the wet, which exhibited limbs of a gigantic size, well adapted for working, running, or kicking. The men also bore the same characteristics; and we could scarcely forbear concluding, the human race was of a superior size.

LANCASTER.

ELEVEN miles, has about eleven streets, sixteen hundred and eleven houses, of stone, and nine thousand and thirty inhabitants; is a genteel place, and abounds with elegant buildings; but the streets are narrow, according to the old fashion of street-making. Our ancestors built for themselves; they never thought of posterity. The Castle, which is in good repair, carries the face of antient grandeur. This, and the great church, are together, and on a high hill, which commands an extensive and beautiful view. I saw the foundation of *Wery Wall*, a Roman work, which seems to have surrounded the Castle-hill.

HEYSHAM,

SIX miles, a watering place, its rocky promontory projecting into the sea, inclosed with wood. It has an admirable effect upon the mind, when we burst upon it by turning the corner, in the road, half a mile distant. There are eighty houses, and three hundred and sixty-five inhabitants. It will probably rise into esteem, for here we find united, the mild aspect of England, with the rough hand of Nature which is spread over North Wales. These rude parts are capable of great improvement.

Upon the crown of a rock, joining the church-yard, is a flat, thirty yards diameter, which precipitates into the sea, where stand the remains of a chapel. In this repository of the dead was taken up a stone coffin, which now lies above ground, and seems to fit a corpse five feet ten, and to have stood the test of a thousand years. A hollow is cut in the hard grit, for the head, neck, shoulders, &c.

Upon this bare rock is a level part, six yards by three and a half, in which have been cut six hollows, or coffins, in a row, in the form of the human body, about twelve inches deep, with a groove round each, to admit a lid. This was probably the depositary of one family, who, instead of *sinking*, may be said to *rise* into the grave. The West side of this rock is washed by the waves and elevated about fifty feet above them. These receptacles of the dead look like half a dozen mummies, in rank.

At Heysham we meant to fix our headquarters for bathing; but our road over the sands leading us to *Hest Bank*, we marched, after a stay of two nights.

HEST BANK, AND KENT SANDS

SIX miles along the shore brought us to this place, a small hamlet three miles North of Lancaster, of very few houses; but chiefly one, and that for the reception of company, who visit for pleasure, or sea-bathing.

As strangers we felt a small degree of anxiety about crossing the Kent Sands, an arm of the sea, which lay at our feet, and which we designed to attempt the next morning. The Guide told us they were twelve miles over, some said eleven, others nine; but the real truth, I believe, is eight.

We agreed with our landlord to take us over for five shillings, and some grog, though the carrier's price is eighteen pence without grog. Our vehicle was a little cart, in which was slung a chair and cushion that would hold two people, with a bag of straw by way of mat for the feet.

We were drawn by something in the form of a little horse, which had almost learnt to live without eating, and of whose ability we had some doubt.

These sands, to the distant eye, appear level; but are very uneven. Every tide changes their face, and leaves hills and vallies. Whatever marks of feet, or wheels, are left in the vacancy of one tide, are washed out by the next. Nor has the stranger any object before him for a guide, because his journey is curved like a bow. A few bushes are pricked into the sands to direct the traveller; but they are small, and the line is often broken. The springing tide rises about nineteen feet.

The eye, continually moving forwards, and engaged upon the same flat object as the sands are, is apt to cause a giddiness in the head. This was experienced by my daughter, with me in the cart, and the servant who followed the track.

Two rivers, from the mountains, run along the sands, the *Kier*, and the *Kent*, which frequently change their course; sometimes they are several miles asunder, and at others, both run in one bed, according to the caprice of the waves.

We found the water up to the ancles a great part of the way. When we had passed about a mile, we crossed the Kier, a brisk stream, upon a wide and flat bottom, reaching to the calf of the leg. Near the North shore, six or seven miles farther, we crossed the Kent. We requested the Guide, who had passed over and waited for us, to go before. It took the horse full to the knee.

He appeared a civil and intelligent veteran, who had stood the cold blast, had passed between wind and water forty years, and knew to an inch whether his horse must walk or swim. He was extremely willing to attend, and it would have been unkind not to have rewarded him. During our short time together, he gave us the history of his profit, and employment. His annual allowance from Government is ten pounds six and eightpence, and a piece of land for his horse, worth nine pounds more; the rest is the uncertain perquisite of the stranger. His emoluments, he remarked, had much declined since the stage-coaches ran, because they not only conveyed passengers, who would otherwise have rode, but carriages and horsemen generally attended the stage, for their own safety; this we had remarked during our short stay.

The general voice of the country is, "the passage is safe," and I believe a man may pass it a thousand times without injury; but I think, to venture over once in his life for *pleasure* is enough; for, if he is obliged to finish his journey in a given time, there must be danger. As there is no road, he is liable to be lost. He may be caught in a fog, or in the night. If on foot, he may wade half the way, and be retarded; if on horse-back, his horse may fail him, or he fall sick; if in a carriage; it may be break down, and he lamed, any accident brings him into a dangerous situation, besides the evil of being caught in a storm without shelter.

Our landlord, who pretended to understand the passage well, was not, we could perceive, guided so much by his own judgement, as by the mark of the stage-wheels, which had passed an hour before us; and wherever they were obliterated, he could not rest, but turned to the right, or left, till he found them, and rejoiced with us when the Guide came to meet us.

In an hour and forty minutes, however, and five hundred lashes, instead of corn, given to the poor horse, we were not displeased to arrive at the opposite shore. We went so charmed at the situation of *Hest Bank*, that we determined, on our return from the Lakes, and the Wall, to order our chattels from Heysham, make this our abode, and proceed thither by land.

NEWBY-BRIDGE, AT THE FOOT OF WINDERMERE,

EIGHTEEN miles from Hest Bank. At the end of twelve miles, we passed through the little, but beautiful town of Cartmel, in a rich country; there are one hundred and forty houses, and 882 inhabitants, who occupy four streets. The church is noble. The town is the property of Lord John Cavendish, whose residence is near. Six miles from hence to Newby-Bridge, an agreeable inn, and five houses; a sweet spot, nearly surrounded by the water of Windermere, where it quits the name of Lake, and becomes a river, nearly the size of the Derwent at Derby.

I had now to walk up this charming Lake, in one of the finest mornings Nature ever made, upon one of the best roads ever constructed, though uneven, and composed of the best materials the earth could produce.

To form an idea of the scene before me, the stranger may imagine to himself a valley between two mountains, which range parallel to each other, and extend more than twelve miles, and whose summits of barren rock are about four miles asunder. Their declivities are woody, and sometimes rough; sprinkled with farms in high cultivation, of perhaps one hundred acres each, and houses which indicate plenty and ease. The bottom, which is from one to three miles over, is the height of rural beauty, extending to the verge of the Lake, and consisting of woods, fertile meadows, and gentlemen's seats. In this centre lies the charming Lake, whose surface was as smooth, pleasant, and clear, as a looking-glass, with a smiling face before it. Not a breath of air to cause a wrinkle, but a bright sun illuminated the view. If an assemblage of mountains, romantic rocks, extensive prospects, fertile valleys, ornamental woods, elegant seats, with a grand expanse of water, can complete a landscape, it may be found here.

The Lake is said to be ten miles and a half long; I have reason to think it is twelve, and from a quarter of a mile to one mile and a half wide, not varying much from a strait line. The head, near Ambleside, seems as wide as any other part; but the foot, at Newby-Bridge, is narrow.

Exclusive of its original source, which is in the Kirkstone mountains, it is supplied perhaps by a thousand rills from the surrounding eminences, some deserving the name of *River,* some *Cascade*, but all clear as crystal; which proves that this grand reservoir is composed of rock-water. I saw a clear bottom at twelve feet deep.

There are many islands, chiefly on the upper part. One of forty-two acres, the property of Mr. Curwen, converted into pleasure ground, and which merits the name of an earthly paradise. I visited this delightful spot; examined every part, after delivering in my name; and though I could not call it mine, I could enjoy its beauties as well as the owner.

Near the centre, upon a rising ground, is a new and expensive house, which I have heard censured as void of taste; but I see no error except its singularity. We are apt to find fault with the ways of another when they differ from our own; this implies a compliment to our judgment.

In a cove formed by the Lake, and a recess formed by the mountains, is situated the pretty village of *Bowness*, having about forty houses. Here we dined, in the summer-house; took an excursion upon the water to see a boat-race, which collected the whole country; but the rain put a stop to the farce.

Our route still continued up the border of the Mere. I frequently ascended the rocks on my right, to improve my view of this grand expanse of water, which gave me a prospect of six or eight miles. Sometimes the road led me nearly level with the water; at others, one or two hundred yards above it: again, I was within a few yards of its margin, and afterwards found myself three hundred yards distant.

At the head of Windermere, near *Ambleside*, is a fortification, which the people call a *Roman Station*. This is an error into which they have been led by the great Camden; who, became *Amboglana,* a real Roman Station, had some affinity of sound with Ambleside, concluded this was the place; and though it afterwards appeared to appertain to Burdoswald, yet the world could not quit the idea. It probably has been a Roman castle, and the place is extremely well adapted for one, as it commands a pass through the mountains. The buildings are totally gone; and it was with difficulty I could find the remains of the old ramparts and ditches. I apprehend it was one of the out-guards to the Wall.

AMBLESIDE,

FIFTEEN miles, a small scattered market-town, surrounded by romantic views; but the place is without form or comeliness, smothered with mountains; to which I shall add nothing, except my gratitude for the attention paid us.

From hence we ascend a very long and steep hill, called Kirkstone; which, for five miles, is a remarkably rough and stony road. Camden might, with the shadow of plausibility, have derived the name of Ambleside from this road, being so extremely bad, that the traveller can scarcely *amble* along, and, lying by its *side*.

Rising and descending this hill, brought up to Patterdale, where is a pool in the valley, half a mile square, called *Broad-Water*; which, had it been alone, might have excited notice; but, situated between two grand Lakes, Windermere and Ulls-Water, which raise the wonder of the traveller, it excites none.

ULLS-WATER

THIS is the sister lake to Windermere, and, like that, is composed of rock-water, clear as crystal, and well tasted. It is upwards of eight miles long. The average width is perhaps three-quarters of a mile, and the depth from thirty to one hundred and twenty yards. The road is on the left bank, good, and shaded with trees; and the Lake fed by a great number of rills, tumbling from the mountains on the left.

On the right, or opposite bank, the rocky mountains for several miles dip into the water, shew, above, their barren sides, and are strangers to cultivation. They afterwards soften into verdure, are less elevated, with inclosures of beautiful farms down to the lower end, which terminates in a river called the *Emont,* at Pooley-Bridge.

William Hutton at the Twice Brewed

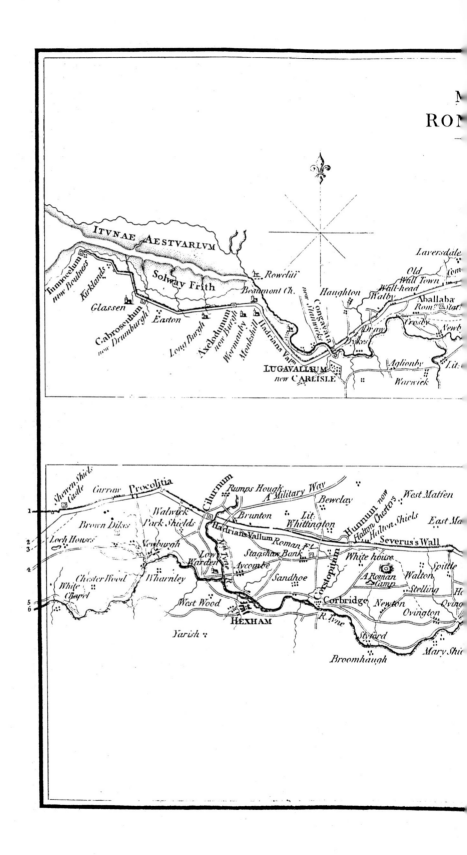

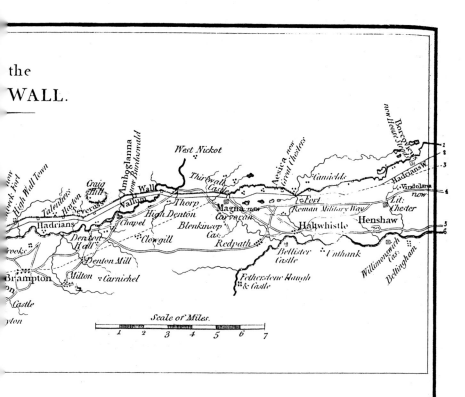

Scale of Miles.

1 2 3 4 5 6 7

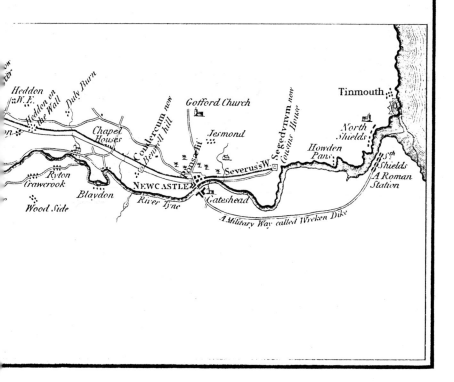

William Hutton being "welcomed" at Rudchester Hall.

On the left side, pursuing our road, we first pass a handsome house, in a recess, or glen, the property of William Mounsey, Esq. a gentleman of wealth and character, on whom the world has conferred the title of *King of Patterdale.*

The next building is Lyulph's Castle, a neat little building; and Garbarrow Park, both the property of the Duke of Norfolk. The Castle is beautiful, the grounds neglected. Then, the Seat of ————— Robinson, Esq.

At Pooley-Bridge, the foot of the Lake, is a circular hill called Dunmallard, upon which are the remains of a Roman castle and fortification. The situation is suitable for guarding the defile. This is another out-guard to the Wall.

Four miles short of Penrith, we pass the charming premises of William Hassell, Esq. of Dalemain.

PENRITH,

TWENTY-FIVE miles from Ambleside, is a handsome and spirited town, with about thirteen streets, six hundred and ninety houses, and 3801 people. It lies in a flat, through which runs a rivulet, and is situated under the Beacon-hill. A mile to the South, runs the Emont.

We read in an old author, that "Penrith "is sixty miles South of Carlisle." The traveller will find it near eighteen. This shews the necessity of correct history.

We visited, like other strangers, *The Giant's Grave,* of which no certain account is given, either by tradition, or history. It lies on the North, within four or five yards of the Church. One stone stands at the head, and another at the feet, not shaped alike, thick as a moderate human body, twelve feet high, and fourteen asunder, ornamented with carvings, which time has nearly obliterated. The sides of the Grave are bordered with semi-circular stones, two feet high, wrought in the same manner.

Blind tradition ascribes this Grave to Sir Ewan Cæsar, said to have been as tall as the columns, who killed the wild boars, and robbers in Inglewood Forest, of which Penrith is a part.

This Grave was opened about forty-five years ago, but nothing found. The stones were replaced. It was opened also about a century prior to that, when, it is said, the large bones of a man's hand were found, and a broad-sword. If this is true, why has the tradition of the inhabitants lost it, and why was not the sword preserved?

The appearance of the stones, however, stamps an age of five hundred years, at least, upon the Grave.

The Castle, upon a delightful spot, is in ruins. This was another guard against that patroling enemy, the Scots; who, in the 19th of Edward the Third, 1346, burnt the town; and again in the next reign, the eighth of Richard the Second.

Richard the Third, while Duke of Gloucester, repaired the Castle; and resided there, to keep the marauders quiet, which had the desired effect.

Here I parted with my daughter, who bore to the left for the residue of the Lakes; and I to the right, for the Wall.

The first eight miles towards Carlisle, is one continued common of excellent land. Pity the times do not call it into cultivation! The road is fine and most beautiful.

CARLISLE,

EIGHTEEN miles, a city with which I was much pleased. There are thirteen streets, thirteen hundred and thirty-eight houses, and 10,220 inhabitants. The streets are rather more spacious than are generally found in ancient cities.

I am now arrived at the long-wished-for Wall. New scenes, and a new task must open. I must appear in the character of an exciseman, with an ink-bottle at my bosom, and a book in my hand; must meet and dine in public with a supervisor, who could not conceive "to what district I belonged," and was too timid, from my appearance, to ask.

I crossed the Eden to Stanwix, a Station, where I slept; then penetrated down to the Boulness, the extremity of the Wall; returned through Carlisle, and Newcastle, to the Wall's end, then down again to Carlisle, where I first entered. But although I travelled the Wall twice, I cannot give two descriptions, lest I confuse the ideas of a reader; but I shall begin at the Wall's end, as all my predecessors have done, and proceed to Boulness.

THE FIRST STATION

SEGEDUNUM OR THE WALL'S END

WHEN part of a building remains, we can sometimes comprehend the whole; but where nothing is left, conjecture is hazardous. This is our present case. No buildings are left in this Station, or any other, to guide the judgment. The spot, now a green pasture, about four acres, three miles and a half below Newcastle, gently declines to the river Tyne; is uneven, as having been covered with buildings. At the top of this green pasture, and parallel with the water, runs Severus's Ditch; so that the Station lies between both.

From the beginning of Severus's Ditch, to the water, the Wall, now gone, must have made a right angle, perhaps eighty yards or more, to the Tyne, so that this cross Wall would also make a right angle with the river. Here stood the Castle. The North corner of the Wall must have been where now stands a cottage, and have entered the water at what they call a trunk, or high timber bridge.

I could not learn from tradition, that time had made any alterations in the tides. As securing this end of the Wall must have been a point of some magnitude, I have no doubt but the Romans took the advantage of low water, to form their butment as deep as circumstances would allow.

Here we see a town full of streets and houses, immured in stone walls; where every man, though a soldier, might, when not upon duty, follow his occupation.

The Bank and Ditch are nearly complete; the last is ten yards wide. Proceeding two hundred yards, it passes a house, late Cousen's, now belonging to John Baddle, Esq. Then Slate's house, to a stile in the valley. Now we rise a hill, with the Wall under the very path we tread. The ditch twelve yards wide. Along a close called Old Walker's-Hill. Byker's Hill. A hedge now runs in the Ditch, a part of which, this year, for the first time, is levelled, and converted into a bed of potatoes, which the proprietors will allow gratis, during three years, to any one who will level, and improve the ground. This is the taste of the neighbourhood for the grandest piece of antiquity in the whole Island.

The Ditch now leaves a windmill close on the right, crosses the road from Newcastle to Shields, about thirty yards North of the toll gate. Goes down the steep hill called Ewsburn, and up to another windmill. Over Shield-field, where, by the name, I suppose a mile-castle has stood, and where the whole is invisible.

We now enter Newcastle, leaving a small part of the town on the right, or North side; but inclosing the principal, and perhaps the whole, when the works were erected. Its passage through these premises is unseen; but it must have been up and down steel hills, till we arrive at Pandon Gate.

During this space of three miles and a half, Severus's Ditch is plainer, nearly all the way, than could be expected in so populous a country. Not the least remains of the Wall, Castles, or Turrets, are to be seen.

At the Wall's end the first cohort had their station.

THE SECOND STATION

PONS ÆLII; NOW NEWCASTLE

HERE I must follow my predecessors, who all through this populous town groped their way in the dark. Busy life ruins antiquity. The faithful Warburton will lead me along this crowded place, where nothing of the Roman is seen; after which I shall be able to walk alone, and perhaps correct my leader.

Though we are arrived at Pandon-gate I apprehend we are not arrived at the Station, but a gate in the town wall, where a turret of the Roman Wall once stood. Pandon, in the time of the Romans, and for ages after, was a distinct village, and given to Newcastle by Edward the First.

Warburton proves that Severus's Wall lies a little to the North of St. Nicholas's church; that the Wall, which passes through the church porch, was the Eastern wall of the Station itself, and that of Severus was the Northern; thus having found two walls of this great square, the other two will follow. He justly allows the medium of a station to be an area of one hundred and thirty six yards square; which, in this case, will reach near the present castle. This points out the Station.

"There are," says my hostess, where I applied for a dinner, "some gentlemen to dine here: should you have any objection to dine with them?"

"Not the least, Madam. I am open to all kinds of company."

My landlord afterwards applied: "Perhaps, Sir, you would chuse to dine in this room alone, upon a dish of fish, and a beef steak?"

"No. I have agreed with my landlady to dine with some gentlemen."

I waited longer than the promise; saw dinner taken in; but no notice taken of me. Disappointment is irksome. "Why am I not," said I to the waiter, "summoned to dinner?" "I will inform you." – The notice came.

I found seven gentlemen fully employed, and a niche left for an eighth.

I was treated with a distant respect; and a small degree of awe governed the whole board.

Dinner over; they requested me to return thanks. Which done; – "You seem, gentlemen, to take me for a clergyman; but I assure you I am in a far preferable state; for I am a *freeman*, which a great part of the Clergy are not. I have nothing to expect from any man but common civility, which I wish to return with interest; but he who is under promises, expectations, or even wishes, his sentiments perhaps may not be his own, and he cannot be deemed free."

Their countenances brightened.

"I have," says one of the gentlemen, "seven relations in the Church."

"Then, Sir, if you are an independent man, are not you the happiest of eight?"

It seemed, their apprehensions of my black dress, from which they were glad to be freed, had nearly deprived me of a dinner.

One of the gentlemen gave, "The King's friends!" To this, though I am no votary for healths, I made no objection; for a friend will not lead a man wrong. But afterwards entering upon indelicate healths, which neither suited the prayer they had requested, nor my pursuits, I withdrew.

The Wall passes near the West gate, and proceeds on our right towards the turnpike. Not many yards before we reach the gate, it crosses the road, and passes through an inclosure, twenty yards on our left; and not through the Quarry-house, which is close to the turnpike road on our right.

The works of Agricola and Hadrian, forty yards more to the left, make their appearance for the first time; but in a faint degree. These works run twenty yards South of Elswick windmill, a little short of the first mile-stone; and Severus's Wall is the very turnpike road on which we tread; it is the great, beautiful, and the famous Roman military way, first formed, I believe, by Agricola, improved by Severus, and brought into its present state by George the Second; and though it does not attend the whole line of the Wall, it communicates between Newcastle and Carlisle. I shall continue to walk for many miles upon the Wall as part of the turnpike road, with small variations, and Severus's Ditch at my right elbow.

We leave, on the right, Fenham Lodge, the seat of William Orde, Esq.; and on the left, that of Robinson Bowes, Esq.

All our Historians have failed in two points: they have not given us the dimensions of the mile-castles, which always joined the Wall, and were from twenty-two to twenty-four yards square; nor distinguished the works of Agricola from those of Hadrian; but have confused both, under the name of the latter.

There were four different works in this grand barrier, performed by three personages, and at different periods. I will measure them from South to North, describe them distinctly, and appropriate each part to its proprietor; for, although every part is dreadfully mutilated, yet, by selecting the best of each, we easily form a whole; from what *is* we can nearly tell what *was*. We must take our dimensions from the original surface of the ground.

Let us suppose a ditch, like that at the foot of a quickset hedge, three or four feet deep, and as wide. A bank rising from it, ten feet high, and thirty wide in the base. This, with the ditch, will give us a rise of thirteen feet at least. The other side of this bank sinks into a ditch ten feet deep, and fifteen wide, which gives the North side of this bank a declivity of twenty feet. A small part of the soil thrown out on the North side of this fifteen feet ditch, forms a bank three feet high, and six wide, which gives an elevation from th bottom of the ditch, of thirteen feet. Thus our two ditches, and two mounds, sufficient to keep out every rogue but he who was determined not to be kept out, were the work of Agricola.

The works of Hadrian invariably join those of Agricola. They always correspond together, as beautiful parallel lines. Close to the North side of the little bank I last described, Hadrian sunk a ditch twenty-four feet wide, and twelve below the surface of the ground; which, added to Agricola's three feet bank, forms a declivity of fifteen feet on the South, and on the North, twelve. Then follows a plain of level ground, twenty-four yards over, and a bank exactly the same as Agricola's, ten feet high, and thirty in the base; and then he finishes, as his predecessor began, with a small ditch of three or four feet.

Thus the two works exactly coincide; and must, when complete, have been most grand and beautiful. Agricola's works cover about fifty-two feet, and Hadrian's about eighty-one; but this will admit of some variation.

The annexed Plate shows,

1. Agricola's Work, with the number of feet.   2. Agricola and Hadrian united.

3. Severus's Wall and Ditch in profile.

Severus's works run nearly parallel with the other two; lie on the North, never far distant; but may be said always to keep them in view, running a course that best suited the judgement of the maker. The nearest distance is about twenty yards, and greatest near a mile, the medium forty or fifty yards.

They consist of a stone wall eight feet thick, twelve high, and four, the battlements; with a ditch to the North, as near as convenient, thirty-six feet wide and fifteen deep. To the Wall were added, at unequal distances, a number of Stations, or Cities, said to be eighteen, which is not perfectly true; eighty-one castles, and three hundred and thirty castelets, or turrets, which I believe is true: all joining the Wall.

Exclusive of this Wall and ditch, these Stations, castles, and turrets, Severus constituted a variety of roads yet called *Roman Roads*, twenty-four feet wide, and

Fig.1. AGRICOLA'S WORK, with the number of feet.

Fig.2. AGRICOLA, and HADRIAN, united.

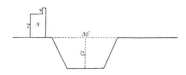

Fig.3. SEVERUS'S WALL, and DITCH, in Profile.

Part of the Wall near BENWELL HILL

with an Apple Tree growing upon its Summit.

eighteen inches high in the centre, which led from turret to turret, from one castle to another, and still larger, and more distant roads from the Wall, which led from one Station to another, besides the grand military way before mentioned, which covered all the works, and no doubt was first formed by Agricola, improved by Hadrian, and, after lying dormant fifteen hundred years, was made complete in 1752.

I saw many of these smaller roads, all overgrown with turf: and, when on the side of a hill, they are supported on the lower side with edging stones.

Thus Agricola formed a small ditch, then a bank and ditch, both large, and then finished with a small bank.

Hadrian joined to this small bank a large ditch, then a plain, a large mound, and then finished with a small ditch.

Severus followed nearly in the same line, with a wall, a variety of stations, castles, turrets, a large ditch, and many roads. By much the most laborious task. This forms the whole works of our three renowned Chiefs.

THE THIRD STATION

CONDERCUM; NOW BENWELL HILL

I HAVE now travelled five miles and a half from the Wall's end; two from Newcastle; and arrived by the military way upon a very considerable eminence, suitable for a Roman Station. Severus's ditch is close on my right, and I upon the foundation of the Wall, as part of the turnpike road; its bare stones under my feet are frequently distinguishable from those used for mending the road.

But the Station totally disappears, except a roughness on the ground, which shews what *has* been; while Agricola and Hadrian's works lie on my left, between me and the village, which contains two hundred and three houses, and nine hundred and fifty-one people.

The Station was very large. The corners, rather canted off, had four entrances answering to the four Cardinal Points. The country and prospects are delightful, and the land good.

I now pass, on my left, another house of Mr. Orde's.

At Denton Dean, or West Denton, situated at the bottom of Benwell Hill, the great road veers a few yards to the right, that is, into Severus's ditch, and gives us for the first time a sight of that most venerable piece of antiquity, *The Wall*, which is six yards South of the road, and twenty short of the brook I am going to pass. The fragment is thirty-six feet long, has three courses of facing stones on one side, and four on the other, and is exactly nine feet thick. An apple-tree grows upon the top, as shewn in the Plate annexed.

The eye can easily trace the line over the water, and unite it to the opposite bank.

Before we leave this village of ninety houses, the Wall again becomes round, and the ditch is at my right elbow.

At the three-mile stone from Newcastle, I leave on my right the seat of Matthew Montague, Esq.

Hadrian's work is now fifty yards on my left.

At the fourth mile-stone, I arrive at Chapel-house, then Castle Steads, where there has no doubt been a mile castle; the situation, as well as the name, corroborates the remark. Fifty yards on my left, down a green pasture, run, in bold figures, the united works of Agricola and Hadrian, dressed in about half their antient grandeur; and, having this clue, we can trace them over the inclosures for many miles.

A little short of the fifth mile-stone is Wallbottle.

At the stone, Hadrian is thirty yards on my left, I upon the Wall.

Newburn Dean is nearly at the sixth mile-stone. Here, climbing a bank, to gain a better view of my valuable companions, I stumbled, and, to save myself, caught at a hawthorn hedge, when, like a Knight of Ulster, I bore the bloody hand.

Pass Throcklow. My two friends Agricola and Hadrian are forty yards on my left.

At the seventh mile-stone is Hadden-on-the-Wall. The road here, as is usual at a village, takes a small turn to the right; it goes up the bank, and leaves Severus's ditch close to my left, and his Wall a yard high; but in a confused heap. There must have been here a mile castle. One hundred yards passed, I again tread the Wall, with the ditch on my right.

Near the eighth mile-stone is the seat of Calverley Bewick, Esq. Here Hadrian assumes a little more consequence; and now we finish our third Station.

THE FOURTH STATION

VINDOBALA; NOW RUTCHESTER

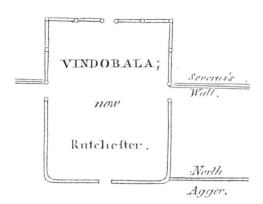

SEVERUS's Wall seems to pass *through* this Station. What remains is a close, joining the road, of five acres, now in grass, and eminently situated; carries the strong marks of former buildings, and still stronger of its ramparts. The platform of this grand Station is complete.

I have all along inquired for turrets; but might as well have inquired among the stars. I was given to understand, that part of one was remaining here. The master told me, "I might find it at the back of his buildings."

Upon examining something like a cow-house, I perceived a small part was Roman work, which might have been part of the butment of the castle, but could not be a turret, for they always stood in front.

> I saw old Sir at dinner sit,
> Who ne'er said, "Stranger, take a bit,"
> Yet might, although a Poet said it,
> Have sav'd his beef, and rais'd his credit.

This old City and suburbs were extensive, and lie in the junction of four roads. Down in the valley, at the ninth milestone, I come to a cottage worth twenty shillings a year.— "Pray what is the name of your place?" "High Seats." "What, because of its *low* situation? You have found a place in history, only from a dignified name."

Here the General, and the Emperor, wear so strong a feature, that all their works may be traced sixty yards on my left.

I am now arrived at Harlow Hill, ten miles and a half from Newcastle, remarkably high. I again bear to the right, and tread, through the town-street, on Severus's ditch, the Wall passing through the houses on my left.

On the highest part stood a mile castle, now a garden, surrounded by its own rampart, very plain. I was shewn a large ash tree, which grew upon the very Wall, recently blown up by the root, and now rears up like a round pancake, eight feet high, and has drawn after it a ton of stones from the Wall, still clinging and interwoven with the root. A brother tree stands near it, waiting for another blast.

The road is charming. The traveller views it two miles each way. It appears like a white ribbon upon a green ground.

Soliciting a bed, I was ushered into a parlour, where sat three gentlemen. I did not conceive I had a right to intrude, so took my place at the greatest distance. A suspicious silence immediately surrounded their little table. As I never made a secret of myself, or the plan I was pursuing, I endeavoured to introduce a communication, for truth makes a wonderful impression upon the mind; when, after an hour or two's chat, one of them remarked, "You are the most agreeable companion I have met with; but, I do assure you, when you first entered, I took you for a spy employed by Government."

They cordially gave me an invitation to their houses; but time would not allow.

It does not appear that dishonesty is totally expunged from the Wall; for though my gloves were deposited where they ought to have been safe, yet I found that some person had made free with them.

The inhabitants remarked, that their elevated station exposed them to violent storms of wind and rain; and that if any snow was left upon the earth, it might be found there.

At the eleventh mile-stone is the village of Wall-houses: there are five. Severus, distinct as before; and Hadrian, thirty yards on the left, but faint. Here must have been a Mile castle. Now a young grove fills Severus's ditch, whith will tend to preserve it.

At the twelfth mile-stone, Agricola is bold, and Severus perfect.

At the thirteenth, High-wall house.

And at the fourtèenth stone, we pass by Sir Edward Blacket's, who is the proprietor of all the works of the General and the two Emperors; and who has converted a *little* farm-house into a *little* castle; so that our favourite banks and ditches have not lost their warlike appearance.

Hadrian, fifty yards on my left, is very conspicuous; I, upon Severus's Wall, and his ditch on my right.

At the fifteenth mile-stone, we pass Halton Shields, a village of twelve houses. I rapped at some doors, tried the latch at others, and hollowed at all; but I believe not a soul was left within, the fine hay-day had emptied the village.

I now enter a common, where the two partners appear in bold and broken lines.

Severus, through the long line of the Wall, seems to chuse the high ground, perhaps the better to observe the approach of an enemy; and Agricola the low, for the benefit of water to supply his ditches; but I was surprised, at the close of the Station, to observe this rule was reversed; for Agricola passes over a steep on my left, and the other seems obliged to take the low ground on which I tread. Perhaps Agricola durst not attempt the swamp; which Severus was obliged to do, as the other had left him no alternative.

THE FIFTH STATION

HUNNUM; NOW HALTON CHEFTERS

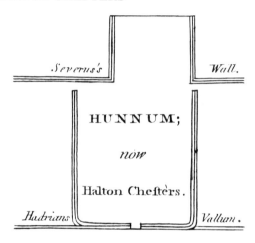

FROM whence Halton Hall derives its name, the antient seat of the Carnabys.

I am eighteen miles from the Wall's end, fifteen and a half from Newcastle, and seven from the last Station. I passed through the centre of this Station without knowing it, till an intelligent gentleman set me right. It is near the foot of the hill I just now mentioned; is flat, which is uncommon for a Station; seems less rough than some other Stations, owing perhaps to its being more cultivated, for it was now covered with standing corn. Severus's Wall passes through the centre of this Station.

The moment I saw it, Severus appeared to have been cramped in his design, that he was obliged to take the low ground, because his predecessor had before taken the high; and, as he could not go behind him, was obliged to proceed over the verge of the swamp.

Rising a long and gentle hill, I was shewn what was once a Mile castle, now a piece of wheat in the open field.

One hundred yards more brings us to Port Gate; that is, two roads cross each other at right angles, both Roman. One is the Watling-street, which, I have no doubt, was made first; the other, the line of the Wall upon which I tread. This being formed after the other, a kind of gate-way, or thoroughfare, was left in the Wall, to facilitate a passage: hence the name.

See in the annexed Plate, a profile of the Roman Wall and Vallum near this Gate, as it appeared in Warburton's time, 1722.

I now travel over a large common, still upon the Wall, with its trench nearly complete. But what was my surprise when I beheld, thirty yards on my left, the united works of Agricola and Hadrian, almost perfect! I climbed over a stone wall to examine the wonder; measured the whole in every direction; surveyed them with surprise, with delight, was fascinated, and unable to proceed; forgot I was upon a wild common, a stranger, and the evening approaching. I had the grandest works under my eye, of the greatest men of the age in which they lived, and of the most eminent nation then existing; all which had suffered but little during the long course of sixteen hundred years. Even hunger and fatigue were lost in the grandeur before me. If a man writes a book upon a turnpike road, he cannot be expected to move quick; but, lost in astonishment, I was not able to move at all.

Upon this common, which is very high ground, I more than once observed some of the facing stones of Severus's Wall under my feet, just as the Romans placed them, which proves that the road is raised so high, as to bury some part of the Wall; this simple sight I could not observe without surprise and pleasure.

At St. Oswald's the road turns a little to the left, for a few yards, and leaves the Wall to the right; but very soon crosses it again.

Had I been some months sooner, I should have been favoured with a noble treat; bat now that treat was miserably soured.

At the twentieth mile-stone, I should have seen a piece of Severus's Wall seven feet and a half high, and two hundred and twenty four yards long: a sight not to be found in the whole line. But the proprietor, *Henry Tulip,* Esq. is now taking it down, to erect a farm-house with the materials. Ninety-five yards are already destroyed, and the stones fit for building removed. Then we come to thirteen yards which are standing, and overgrown on the top with brambles.

A piece of the Wall, as it still appears at this place, is shewn in the annexed Plate.

A Piece of Severus's Wall as it now appears near
ST OSWALD'S.

The next forty yards were just demolished; and the stones, of all sizes, from one pound to two hundred weight, lying in one continued heap, none removed.

The next forty yards are standing, seven feet high.

Then follows the last division, consisting of thirty-six yards, which is sacrificed by the mattock, the largest stones selected, and the small left. The facing stones remain on both sides. This grand exhibition must be seen no more. How little we value what is daily under the eye!

Here was a fine opportunity for measuring. The foundation was one foot below the surface of the ground, and consisted of two courses of stone, each six inches thick, extending to the width of six feet and a half. The second course set off three inches on each side, which reduced the foundation to six feet, and the third three inches of a side more, reducing the Wall to five feet and a half, its real thickness here.

Profile of the Remains of SEVERUS'S **WALL** .

The plate here given represents a profile of the remains of the Wall as it now appears at this place. The foundation of which is laid in the native earth, the rest is cemented with mortar.

The soil being afterwards thrown up on each side of the Wall two feet high, caused the foundation to be three feet deep.

I desired the servant with whom I conversed, "to give my compliments to Mr. Tulip, and request him to desist, or he would wound the whole body of Antiquaries. As he was putting an end to the most noble monument of Antiquity in the whole Island, they would feel every stroke. If the Wall was of *no* estimation, he must have a mean opinion of me, who would travel six hundred miles to see it; and if it *was*, he could never merit my thanks for destroying it."

"Should he reply, 'The property is mine, and I have a right to direct it as I please;' it is an argument I can regret, but not refute."

I am now descending a hill of some magnitude, called *Wall Fell*, and I am within half a mile of the river of North Tyne. Could I follow the line of the Wall, it would lead me to what was once the Roman Bridge over that river; the foundation of which, I was given to understand, I might see if I would wade; but as I could not do one, nor wished to do the other, I submitted to the turnpike road, and the present bridge, which perhaps is half a mile above that of the Romans, and which obliged me to quit the line of the Wall for two miles.

And here I must be allowed to call in question the wisdom of the moderns, who have erected a bridge at twice the expence; for the water is here twice as wide, two hundred and fifty feet; and, by quitting the Roman line, caused the traveller to march two miles instead of one. But private interest is known to prevent public good.

The eye can easily carry the works of the three great men over the water, across the valley; and up one inclosure of perhaps two hundred yards, five or six acres; and in the next close, we see it terminate in our Fifth Station, full of hills and hollows, from which it has acquired the modern name of Chester Holes.

THE SIXTH STATION

CILURNUM; NOW WALWICK CHESTERS

I AM not far from the twenty-second mile-stone, between Newcastle and Carlisle. The inclosure where this City stood seems, like the other Stations, to be five or six acres; but is in reality an oblong of 400 feet by 570, nearly eight acres. It is in grass, very uneven, owing to former use, and rather elevated, though near the bottom of high ground. But the Romans were obliged to fix here, or they could not guard the river.

The annexed plan of this Station, with part of the plan of Severus's Wall and Hadrian's Vallum, shews how they were connected at the Stations; and their mutual relation to one another must have been one entire united defence or fortification.

The Banks, Wall, and Trenches, having crossed the Water of North Tyne and passed this Station, kept together, and proceed by the spacious seat of Nathaniel Clayton, Esq. who holds the honour of being proprietor of the works of two Emperors, and the Bonaparte of the day.

Rising the hill to Walwick, the village is delightful, and the prospect most charming. At the corner of a garden-wall, I saw a beautiful pedestal, panelled, moulded, and fluted, in perfection, two feet by eighteen inches; no doubt a Roman relick, degraded to a shabby prop, as a thing of no value.

We pass the seat of Henry Tulip, Esq.

The works of Agricola and Hadrian still continue on my left; but Severus crosses the turnpike road in the village, and appears on my right, a Wall three feet high, but in a rude state, and without facing-stones; for we can easily conceive a wall, levelled with the ground, and seven or eight feet thick, will bear its own rubbish a yard high.

The Emperor and General on my left, in striking characters, are cut through the rock; and the great military way fills up the space between Severus and them.

I am now at the twenty-third mile-stone; the morning delightful, and the parallel lines before me magnificent.

A Plan of Cilurnum, the Roman Station at WALWICK CHESTERS; with part or the Plan of SEVERUS's WALL and HADRIANS VALLUM.

I O M
ET NVMINIBVS
AVG COH · IT V
NGRORVM
MIL · CVIRÆ E
ST QVERIVS
SVPERSTIS
PRAEFECIVS

Roman Altar, now the Mantle tree at a Farm-house at
HOUSE STEADS

Profile of the Mountains at BRADLEY.

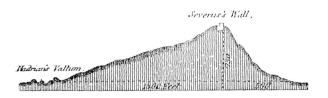

At the twenty-fourth mile-stone, I still have Severus's trench, and what remains of the Wall, on my right, and Hadrian's works on my left, with the military way on which I tread, only twelve yards wide, between, which fills up the space. Thus am I hemmed in by dignity, upon the best of roads, upon elevated ground, with extensive prospects, in a country thinly inhabited, surrounded with commons, or with inclosures of fifty or a hundred acres each, but without trees or hedges, and where the face of the earth seems shaved to the quick. Yet in this solitary place, where foot seldom treads, I enjoy the company of three valuable friends, Agricola, Hadrian, and Severus.

At Towertay, Severus's Wall appears in more dignity, with two or three courses of facing-stones; but generally, in this part of my route, with only the rude stones lying upon the foundation.

THE SEVENTH STATION

PROCOLITIA; NOW CARRAWBURGH

THIS Seventh City upon the Wall lies upon an open and elevated spot. A farm-house stands exactly upon the works of Hadrian and Agricola. The Station joins the house, is six or seven acres, in grass, exceedingly hilly, declaring the former actions of busy life, and is yet secured by its original ramparts.

The Wall here makes a bend, as if with design to inclose this spot. It seems, by the roughness of the ground, to have had a suburb to the West, where a well, or rather a Roman Bath, has been found seven feet square, quoined with stone.

I was treated here with great civility, when they found I was neither Exciseman, Spy, nor Methodist Preacher.

A Roman stone, which graced the old Castle, graces the internal wall of the present house; a man's chubby face, ten inches square, without inscription, but is ornamented with drapery.

Here the bold ruins of all the works appear.

As the twenty-fifth mile-stone, Hadrian is forty yards on my left, and Severus close to my right, not very conspicuous.

Upon the hill rising to Carrow, the foundation of Severus's Wall is seen, with a boundary hedge growing upon it; and in one place three or four courses of facing-stones appear for about fifteen yards. The other two, thirty yards on my left.

Pass by Carrow, a single house, on the summit of an eminence, where must have been a Mile castle; it lies between Hadrian and Severus's works.

At the twenty-sixth mile-stone, the General and the Emperor are seen in formidable beauty; while Severus is rather sinking, yet noble. Upon the hill, twenty-six miles and a half, all the mounds and trenches appear in strong lines.

At the twenty-seventh mile-stone, the *two* appear in bold and noble characters. But now I must quit this beautiful road, and the more beautiful scenes of cultivation, and enter upon the rude of Nature, and the wreck of Antiquity; for this grand military way bears to the left, and the Wall to the right.

I am now thirty miles and a half from the Wall's end, and twenty-seven from Newcastle; have been close to the Wall all the way, except as passing the Tyne; and, for about twenty miles of the above space, have trod upon the very Wall, as constituting part of the great military way, though unobserved by the common passenger, with Severus's trench at my right elbow, generally in a bold style. The works of Agricola and Hadrian mostly visible on my left; but always carried through inclosures.

The two works now must separate, and be a mile, or near it, asunder for the next ten miles; for Agricola and Hadrian humbly pursue the lower grounds, while Severus climbs the rocky mountains.

I follow the Wall. It now appears six feet high; but divested of facing-stones, and in a rude heap. Here I find the platform of a Castle, whose wall is six courses high, and about four feet long.

Travelling three hundred yards, I come to the foundation of another building joining the Wall; but levelled, in the form of a bow, the Wall supposed the string. It could not be a Mile castle; perhaps a place of arms.

Half a mile before I come to Shewenshields are the remains of a Castle, twenty-two yards by thirty; an entrance on the East, South, and West, with a foss on three sides, remarkably bold, and on the fourth the Wall. It has had four Turrets, one at each corner. Here I observe Agricola and Hadrian creeping modestly along the valley below.

Severus runs along, from one to three feet high, all confusion, mounting every craggy precipice it can find, and, from the prodigious declivity on the North, needs not ditch; while Agricola and Hadrian beautifully proceed over a small eminence below, five hundred yards South, where their works, or rather Agricola's, joins a large fort sixty yards square, once a Castle.

Here Severus's Wall runs crooked, and catches the precipices wherever it can. About a mile after we quit the great road, we arrive at a gap in the mountian, an inlet to the famous Moss Troopers; who here broke through the Wall in bodies, for plunder and blood. The Mosses are the meadows on the North below; which, though rather in an uncultivated state, are passable.

A small Castle stood in the meadow, near the foot of the hill, to prevent the Picts, and afterwards the Moss Troopers, by guarding the pass, the remains of which appear. Tradition says, it was built by King *Ethel*, which must be an abridgment of Ethelrick, Ethelfrid, or Ethelred, for they were all Saxon Kings of Northumberland. It was not likely to be the first or last, for they reigned but four years each. It must then have been Ethelfrid, who reigned twenty-three years, was a spirited prince, and fought with the North Britons. We may date the erection of this Castle between the year 593 and 617. But, whoever was the architect, he knew but little of Castle-building. It ought to have been placed upon one of the limbs of the pass.

I am now upon a place called Shewenshields, about twenty-eight miles from Newcastle, once a Mile castle, now a dreary farm of 2070 acres, occupied by Mr. Matthew Magnay, who paid me every attention. It includes the Mosses on the North of the Wall, and the rocks on the South, and is better adapted to the teeth than the plough.

Mr. Magnay took me to a small gutter in the rock upon his farm, which bears the name *Cats Cover*, (as small as would admit a cat). Here the Scots bored under the Wall so as to admit the body of a man; for, if one could get through, a thousand might follow; for there was nobody either to watch, or oppose them. The Britons must have been very supine; for two days labour of three men would have made this narrow pass so secure, that the more they bored, the deeper they would have penetrated into the rocky mountain.

The elevation of Shewenshields house is remarkable; it commands an amazing view, part of which is the Cheviot Hills. Mr. Magnay asked me, "if I would sit in King Ethel's chair?" to which I assented. He took me to the top of a precipice fifty feet high, close behind the Wall; from the bottom of which rose a perpendicular rock, rather in the form of a chimney, much higher than we stood, and six feet from the precipice; it had a set-off, which resembled the seat and back of a chair; but neither Ethel, nor any one else, ever sat in it.

The Wall is here six or seven feet high, but in confusion; keeps a zigzag line merely to follow the precipice. I requested my friend Magnay to conduct me to the famous *Busy Gap,* about twenty-nine miles from Newcstle; so called from the frequency of the Picts and Scots breaking through this gap, and surprizing the Romans and Britons, and afterwards of the Moss Troopers. This I also found to be a break in the mountain over which the Wall ran, now filled up by a common-field gate, two yards and a half wide. It lies one mile beyond Shewenshields.

The human mind is apt to rise into the wonderful. Most tales are stretched *a little* beyond what they ought to bear. How often have we "never seen such a thing in our lives!" "Every thing in the world" often rings in our ears. Something like this is the case of the Moss Troopers. "They could pass over bogs which nobody else could. They burrowed into rocks and holes which none could find out, and places where none durst approach."

The simple truth is, they have no rocks or holes to burrow in, or bogs to pass, which another could not. No doubt they were able-bodied men, as all thieves ought to be, or they would not be fit for the calling. Their manner was, to assemble in a body, break the Wall in the weakest, or most convenient place, fight, run, burn your house, or drive away your cattle, as occasion offered. The advantage would always lie on the strongest side.

As I passed through Penrith, I paid my respects to John Hutton, Esq. (perhaps my relation). In our discourse he remarked, "That one of his ancestors, a stout man, returning from Carlisle, met six Scots men driving twenty head of cattle, which they had stolen. Being armed himself, and they having only bludgeons, he drew his sword, fell furiously upon them, wounded some, made the whole body disperse, and recovered the prey, which he drove back to the owners."

A more dreary country than this in which I now am, can scarcely be conceived. I do not wonder if shocked Camden. The country itself would frighten him, without the Troopers.

As the evening was approaching, and nature called loudly for support and rest, neither of which could be found among the rocks; I was obliged to retreat into the military road, to the only public house, at three miles distance, known by no other name than that of *Twice Brewed*.

"Can you favour me with a bed?"

"I cannot tell till the company comes."

"What, is it club-night?"

"Yes, a club of carriers."

A pudding was then turned out, about as big as a peck measure; and a piece of beef out of the copper, perhaps equal to half a calf.

"You must be so kind as to indulge me with a bed. I will be satisfied with any thing."

"I cannot, except you will sleep with this man" (pointing to a poor sick traveller who had fallen ill upon the road).

"That will be inconvenient."

"Will you consent to sleep with his boy?" (about ten.) "Yes."

Having completed our bargain, and supped, fifteen carriers approached, each with a one-horse cart, and sat down to the pudding and beef, which I soon perceived were not too large. I was the only one admitted; and watched them with attention, being highly diverted. Every piece went down as if there was no barricade in the throat. One of those pieces was more than I have seen eaten at a meal by a moderate person. They convinced me that eating was the "chief end of man." The tankard too, like a bowl lading water out of the well, was *often emptied, often filled.*

My landlady, however, swerved from her agreement; for she found me a whole bed to my wish.

THE EIGHTH STATION

BORCOVICUS; NOW HOUSE-STEADS

I AM now thirty miles from Newcastle. Becoming a gainer at *Twice Brewed* by a broken promise, which is seldom the case, I retreated next morning over a Moss to my favourite pursuit, which brought me to House-Steads, the grandest Station in the whole line. In some Stations the Antiquary feeds upon shells, but here upon kernels. Here lie the remains of antient splendour in bold characters.

The line, as usual, proceeds over the crags, which leave a precipice fifty feet high on the North. At the bottom are three pools. The Wall is six or seven feet high; but miserably broken, and continues in the same style six or seven miles, a heap of rubbish. In some parts only three feet high, and occasionally shews five or six courses of facing stones.

The Station is, of course, much elevated; declines to the South; the ramparts are plain. A very large Suburb seems to have been added to this populous City , now reduced to one solitary house; the whole about fifteen acres. The curious observer, I believe, may count twenty streets. The population, perhaps, could not be less than two or three thousand souls.

From the melancholy relicks on the spot, it must have been graced with some elegant buildings.

A Temple, no doubt, was one. I saw the square base of a large pillar, with a circular shaft preceeding from it, fourteen inches diameter, curiously moulded. Another of a different form, with a square shaft eighteen inches diameter; noble remains of fifteen hundred years! which loudly declare the days of antient splendour. The Castle stood at the corner, North-West, within the Station; was itself moated round, as were also the Station and the Suburbs, separately.

Joining the Wall, within, are the remains of a court of Justice, about twelve yards long, and six wide. In the West corner was the Judge's seat, six feet diameter, and quoined with stone, ten courses of which remain. It is not easy to survey these important ruins without a sigh: a place once of the greatest activity, but now a solitary desert; instead of the human voice, is heard nothing but the winds.

In the farm house down in the valley, the jamb which supports the mantle-tree is one solid stone, four feet high, two broad, and one thick, complete as in the day the workman left it, as in the Plate here annexed; which may be also found in Warburton's History of the Wall, Plate III. p.60; and in Gough's improved edition of Camden's Britannia, 1789, vol. III. Plate xvii. p.245.

There are also many curious figures, all Roman, in this Station.

I had now the severe task of creeping up rocks, and climbing stone walls, not well adapted to a man who has lost the activity of youth.

As the works of the two celebrated Chiefs continued in view, and being invited by a single house in the valley, of some magnitude, called *Bradley Hall*, where I might gain knowledge; I descended the hill, to tread upon that venerable ground; a distance Warburton calls 600 yards, perhaps good measure. I found them all very distinguishable, though in mowing grass, and in a perfect swamp.

The annexed Plate shews a profile of the Mountains at Bradley Hall, on top of which runs Severus's Wall, and Hadrian's Vallum at the bottom.

Entering the Hall, the family, whose name I am sorry I have forgotten, seemed to strive which should treat me with the most kindness. It consisted of a father and mother, two sons, near six feet each, and two beautiful Sacharissa's, who though aiding the churn, will not, like *Waller's* lovely rose, bloom and *wither* in a desert, but find their way into the busy world.

On the rough rock, opposite Crag Lough, the Wall is three feet high; but deprived of all the facing stones, and bends to avoid the pool. The ditch is in perfection.

At another spot upon this Crag, the Wall is eleven courses high on one side, and from three to five on the other; and, for sixty yards, is eight feet high.

I now consider myself in the middle of the kingdom, between the German Ocean, and the Irish Sea; consequently upon the most elevated ground between both, and distant, in a straight line, by land, about fifty miles from each. We must allow, from the convexity of the Globe, a rise of one hundred and fifty yards; and the mountain on which I stand will perhaps give a rise of forty more. It follows, I am elevated one hundred and ninety yards above the Sea. The prospects are not grand, but extensive, and rather awful. Upon the Great Crag, are three courses of facing stones.

The judicious Warburton "believes, that the works of Hadrian lie at a considerable distance South of this Station, and that they make a small turn at the brook to come at it." But can a thing be brought *near* to what does not exist!

Hadrian was dead long before the appearance of this Station.

THE NINTH STATION

VINDOLANA; NOW LITTLE CHESTERS

I THINK myself bound to place Little Chesters among the Stations, that I may follow my predecessors, and not break their numerical order. Although Roman, and garrisoned by Romans, it does not appear to belong to the works of Severus. It stands near two miles South of the Wall.

Agricola erected Castles adjoining his works; but this stands nearly a mile South of his, therefore it could add no security.

It probably was used as a prison, and this is corroborated by a remark of our writers, "That there was discovered under a heap of rubbish a square room below the ground, strongly vaulted, and paved with large square stones, set in lime; and under this another room, whose roof was supported by rows of square pillars." These two rooms could answer no end but that of a prison.

There are four Stations, of the eighteen, smaller than the rest, which are detached from the Wall, and lie considerably to the South:

Little Chesters;
Carvoran;
Cambeck Fort; and
Watch Cross.

As Little Chesters is the first that occurs, it is necessary to speak of all the four.

Hadrian and Severus could have nothing to do with these. They were most probably the work of Agricola. That he made the banks and ditches I have described in his name, is not doubted. That he erected some Castles it is clear; but, for many ages, all his ramparts, mounds, trenches, and Castles, have gone under the name of Hadrian's.

If he erected Castles and mounds, there must have been roads to communicate with them. It is reasonable then to conclude, that he was the author of all the roads appertaining to his Works.

A Roman road went from Walwick Chesters, directly to Little Chesters, and left *Carrowburgh* and *Housesteads* much on the right. It then proceeded from Little Chesters to *Carvoran,* leaving *Great Chesters* on the right, and directed its course to *Cambeck Fort,* leaving *Burdoswald* to the right, and then took its course to *Watch Cross.* All these four stations lie to the South, totally distinct from Severus's Wall, or Stations Agricola must have formed them for the accommodation of his works.

The road I have described is about eighteen miles; besides many smaller roads, which were connected with his grand undertaking. It may be considered as a string, and Severus's Wall, the bow. It ends in the great military way, and joins Severus's Wall about four miles before we come to Carlisle; in all about twenty-eight miles.

Severus, afterwards, constructed a great number of roads, now to be seen, which branched from this towards the North, and communicated with his Wall, Stations, &c.

The Wall, at Wall-green, takes a small turn, and continues about three feet high, broken as usual: and Severus's Ditch is in high preservation, as we rise the hill to the next Station.

THE TENTH STATION

ÆSICA; NOW GREAT CHEFTERS

THIS Station is elevated as usual, and thirty five miles from Newcastle; is about five acres, very uneven. No buildings remain, except a modern farm-house, all the doors of which I found open, and none to guard the premises but a child, from whom I could gain no intelligence. There was no danger of a thief; for, in this solitary place, he must come a great way to take a little.

The trenches and ramparts are bold, particularly on the West, where they are very large. The appearance of the place, and the idea of past transactions, strike the soul with awe. It appears by the ground, that the buildings have swelled into a Suburb. The marks of a Temple, and Court of Justice, are visible. The Wall, in confusion, is here about three feet high. The swelling banks shew where the Castle stood, and particularly mark the butments.

The General and the Emperor, with mild features, are seen half a mile below, gliding along the valley.

Drawing near Cockmount Hill, four hundred yards forward, and in a high situation, I am frequently favoured with a few courses of facing-stones. Agricola and Hadrian, still half a mile South, in the valley: the reason is, Severus attempts a precipice, if he can. Here the Wall ascends the rocks.

There is a Tumulus in the meadow, near the works of the two great men. Now we come to a Well, made famous because one of the Saxon Kings was baptized here, perhaps without a feast.

We arrive at Wall-town, if a single house deserves the name. On each side the door stands a Roman Altar, used for washing hands, kettles, dishes, &c. and has at last the honour of supporting the dish-clout. I saw one old female, who treated me shily, and heard a younger, who durst not see me; and both, I have reason to think, wished me gone: but, perhaps, I had the most reason to be frightened.

The Wall ascends the rocks. Here Camden was terrified again, at the imaginary houses of the Moss Troopers, and relinquished his examination of the Wall. The name is Walton Crag. I found the ascent so difficult that I sometimes was obliged to crawl on all fours.

Here the Wall having facing-stones on each side, allowed me to take the measure; I found its thickness barely nine feet. In one place, for about two yards, and that upon a sharp declivity, there are eight courses of facing-stones.

THE ELEVENTH STATION

MAGNA; NOW CARVORAN

THIS small Station, thirty-eight miles from Newcastle, seems to belong rather to the works of Agricola, than to those of Severus; or perhaps it belongs to neither, being about three hundred yards South of the nearest.

The situation of the ground is a valley between two hills. Through this valley, and through the Wall, runs the river Tippal, which opening demanded a security to the pass, as well against the Britons as the Scots.

Opposite therefore to Carvoran was erected in after-ages, on the North side of Severus's Wall, Thirlwell Castle *(Thorough Wall)* from the Scots breaking through. The situation of Thirlwell Castle is well chosen, upon an elevated round knob of earth. It is the property of the Earl of Carlisle, and far gone in decay.

Here I met with all the civility even friends could bestow. A little beyond is the mark of a Mile castle, ten yards square.

I have now done with desolate mountains, precipices, and climbing stone walls; which have continued more than ten miles.

Half a mile short of Mumps Hall is a hollow in the mountain called *Stone Gap,* where the Scots broke through. I am now in that part of the Wall which Nature had the least defended; for the river Tippal, mentioned above, falls into the North Tyne. This last running forty miles Eastward, and parallel with the Wall, on the South side, became a kind of guard which prevented the Northern plunderers from penetrating into the country. And, about three miles West of this place, the little surly river Irthing crosses the Wall, and flows into the Eden; which, running Westward to Carlisle about eighteen miles, became an out-guard to the other part of the Wall. The intermediate space of three miles between the North Tyne, aided by the Tippal on the left, and the Irthing feeding the Eden on the right, became a fine opening for plunder.

I now cross a small rivulet called *Poltross,* which gives me an entrance into Cumberland, being forty-four miles from the Wall's end, forty and a half from Newcastle, about sixteen and a half from Carlisle, and twenty-nine and a half from Boulness.

The Wall, close to my left, runs along a meadow, is about a yard high, in confusion, has a hedge growing upon it, till it reaches the East bank of the Irthing, where it stops. The West bank is a precipice, which Warburton calls forty yards perpendicular: perhaps he is right. The Wall undoubtedly went to the foot of this hill, and must end there; for the side is too steep, I think, to admit a Wall; but its broken end is visible on the top.

I had this river to cross, and this mountain to ascend; but did not know how to perform either. I effected a passage over the river by the assistance of stones as large as myself, sometimes in, and sometimes out; but with difficulty reached the summit of the precipice by a zig-zag line, through the brambles, with a few scratches.

At the top I had a view of the Wall where it was broken off to the foundation. It measured seven feet exactly.

THE TWELFTH STATION

AMBOGLANNA; NOW BURDOSWALD

TRADITION says it derived its name from Oswald, King of Northumberland, who was surprized by his enemies while fishing in a neighbouring pool. It could not be Oswald, who lost his life in battle with Penda, the Mercian King, at Oswestry. If there is any truth in the tradition, it must have been Oswald, who was raised to the throne of Northumberland by a faction, about the year 800, and was deposed after a reign of twenty-eight days.

When I entered the house of Mr. Bowman, who is the proprietor, and occupier, of these once imperial premises, I was received with that coldness which indicates an unwelcome guest, bordering upon a dismission; for an ink-bottle and book are suspicious emblems. But, as information was the grand point in view, I could not, for trifles, give up my design; an expert angler will play with his fish till he can catch him.

With patience, with my small stock of rhetoric, and, above all, the simplicity of my pursuit, which was a powerful argument, we became exceedingly friendly; so that the family were not only unwilling to let me go, but obliged me to promise a visit on my return. They gave me their best; they wished it better. I had been, it seems, taken for a person employed by Government to examine private property, for the advancement of taxation.

I assured them, that my journey rose from the idle whim of an Antiquary; that I had employed *myself,* and that my right hand must pay my left.

The Station at Burdoswald, forty-three miles from Newcastle, and fifteen from Carlisle, contains five or six acres, joins the Wall, like other Stations, on the North. All the Roman buildings are down; but the marks of many appear. The ground will tell us what has been laid upon it. Some have been the turrets of the Castle. One a prison. Another, twelve yards by five, was designed for the guard. The whole Station is surrounded by a foss. All the entrances are plain. The whole in a high situation.

The Wall here is six feet thick. Mr. Bowman's fold, &c. stand on the very works. I left these worthy people with some concern.

Upon the common, called *Midgham foot,* a little beyond the favourite premises of Burdoswald, the Wall had been recently taken down, and lies in heaps, as if the country could not produce one soul to protect Antiquity. Agricola and Hadrian lie one hundred yards on my left.

I thought I observed the foundation of a turret, but am not certain; I saw, however, forty yards of facing-stones, from five to seven courses high. In another place on the common, called the Banks, I saw eight. All the mounds, the Wall, and the ditches are seen all the way along this common; the Wall four feet high.

At *Bank head,* the foundation of the Wall only is seen; the trench is in perfection; a foot-path runs along the bottom.

I entered a farm-house for intelligence; I was treated with great shyness, till they understood my pursuit. It appeared, they had taken me for a surveyor of land, preparatory to inclosing the commons.

At *Hare hill,* which, by the bye, stands in a valley, the Wall is ten feet high, and five yards long; but the front stones are gone. I viewed this relick with admiration; I saw no part higher; it was within two feet of the battlements. Near this place the Wall is five feet high, with the foundation of a Castle twenty yards square.

Now I find a small part, with three tier of facing-stones, ten yards long, and four feet high, with a new wall added by a gentleman to the old, which will preserve it.

A little farther, the banks and ditch are perfect; and Severus's Wall is built upon the soil thrown out of his own ditch, as is perceptible in many other places.

Over the valley, for the space of two hundred yards, the Wall is four feet high, and a boundary hedge grows upon its top.

Proceeding from Haden, a new Wall is erected upon the spot where the old one stood, with some of its materials; and the remainder are scattered.

I now traverse another common, half a mile over, where all the works are just discernible. Then passing half a mile more, part over watery ground, and the sun down, my limbs told me, I had done enough for the day; and a guide directing me where I might sleep, I applied to the sign of the Cow and Boot, at High Walton, for a bed.

"Sir, we cannot take you in."

"You must be kind enough to assist me, for there is no other place in which I can sleep. Dispose of me how you please, but do not turn me out."

Silence was the answer, which I considered a favourable one. There were, besides the father and mother, six children, chiefly females, and grown up. One of them, a young woman, I was sorry to see, was approaching the grave.

Although a public-house, they had no ale, cyder, porter, beer, or liquors of any kind, or food, except milk, which was excellent; but they treated me with something preferable, Civility.

When I rose the next morning, and asked my worthy landlady, what I had to pay? I found she would be satisfied with only a few pence! Ignorant of the polite art of duping, I found she knew but little of the world.

I laid down two shillings. In surprize, she returned one, and offered to give change for the other. I insisted upon her taking both. Still unwilling, I was obliged to promise to make her a harder bargain at my return.

When a man serves me with his best in time of need, he merits my money and my thanks.

THE THIRTEENTH STATION

PETRIANA; NOW CAMBECK FORT

FIFTY miles from Newcastle, and eight from Carlisle; a modern name, derived from the river Cambeck. The works are wholly gone; for a gentleman, who, like other "wise men from the East," had acquired a fortune in India, recently purchased the estate on which this Castle stood, for thirteen thousand pounds, stocked up the foundation, and erected a noble house on the spot. Other Stations preserve the ruins, but this only the name; and is the first which has been sacrificed to modern taste.

It also bears the name of *Castle Steads,* perhaps the most proper. This small fort stands at so great a distance from all the works, that I can scarcely admit it among the Stations. It could be of no more use to Severus's Wall, than various other fortifications scattered over the country on both sides of the Wall. It might be of rather more use to Agricola. It is the third reputed Station which stands out of the line; and was, I have no doubt, erected by him, and most probably accepted by Severus, and occupied by him as a Station; otherwise, we cannot account for the great vacancy between Burdoswald and Watch Cross, which is more than nine miles; or rather between Burdoswald and Stanwix, which is fourteen miles, and would have been too great a distance between the Stations, a distance no where found. So that between the above two, which line with the Wall, we find two that do not, Cambeck Fort, of which we now treat, and Watch Cross, which follows.

The ground-plot was visible before the purhcase, and is all that was left of the Station. Along the Wall, Severus's ditch with the Works of Agricola and Hadrian may be traced; but the higher we rise in cultivation the more we sink in antiquity. The plough will bury its last remains.

The works now pass Newton, and Old Walton, much in a feeble style, except Severus's trench, which, through the inclosures, makes, and perhaps ever will make, a bold figure.

Wall-*Head*, a single house, in a *low* situation! Here the people viewed me with a suspicious eye when I entered the house, and, I have reason to think, rather wished me out. A book in my hand, and ink-bottle at my breast. "What could I be but a surveyor of land, employed by the landlord, preparatory to a rise of rent!"

But when I could dispel the gloom, and raise a smile, I became a most welcome guest; was received with additional joy, in proportion to the depth they had been let down; was obliged to drink tea, and promise a return of the visit. Thus the civil treatment rose from the removal of an expected injury.

THE FOURTEENTH STATION

ABALLABA; NOW WATCH CROSS

IT is sometimes called *Scaleby Castle*. This is still a less Station, and the least in the line: fifty-three miles from Newcastle, and five from Carlisle; lies more than a mile South of all the works; and for what use placed here by Agricola is uncertain, except to guard a road. This is the fourth Station of the eighteen, which is detached from the Wall.

A Roman road proceeds from Walwick Chesters, already mentioned; takes a course like the string of a bow for twenty-six miles, and then joins the Wall near Wallby. A branch of this road runs up to Thirlwell Castle. It also communicates with Little Chesters, and Carvoran, both detached Stations. The same road extends to two other Out-Stations; for, by passing through Crakes-town, and Burtham, it reaches *Cambeck Fort;* and then, through Newton and Irthington, it reaches *Watch Cross,* proceeds on to Low Crosby, and Wallby, as above.

It is said, the kingdom at the time I am speaking of was full of timber; and that the Romans occasionally cleared it away, to make their roads, and to faciliate a passage for large bodies of men, provisions, &c. which could not, in many places, have been conveyed without.

When they had formed the roads, it became equally necessary to guard them. Hence these four Southern Stations. As a farther security to this long and naked part of the Wall, in after-ages, was erected *Scaleby Castle,* which, like Thirlwell, lies at a small distance North of Severus; this, perhaps, three hundred yards, and Thirlwell, one, which became a tolerable defence.

While the Wall was new, it was well guarded, which insured peace. The principal offices under Severus and his successors frequently procured grants of land, upon which they erected Castles of defence; and, as a gentleman who knew the whole line, remarked to me, they chose the most fertile spots in the country. Scaleby was one of those grants. The Tilliots owned it about the time of King John; then the Pickerings, the Musgraves, the Gilpins; and it is now the property of William Richardson, Esq. of Wallby; but, like the fortifications of the Wall, is in ruins.

I now pass Bleatern, where the Wall is said "to run through mossy ground, and they were obliged to erect it upon piles of wood." But I saw no piles of wood, or mossy ground, though I sought for both, neither an occasion for piles.

Bleatern stands upon elevated ground, able to support a wall without the help of wood; besides, had there been mossy ground, Severus's ditch, in high condition here, would have drained the land for the Wall. I found, however, as much attention paid me, within the house, as I wished.

All the way from Bleatern to Wallby, more than a mile, the common high-way, (not the turnpike road,) is on the Wall itself; with the ditch on my right.

I asked a gentleman, who was amusing himself in his garden by the road, some questions relative to my pursuit; who answered with great civility,

"Will you step in, Sir, and take a glass?"

What man, like me, burnt up by a midday sun, could refuse? Besides I was in a country where I could not purchase. The solicitation repeated, I accepted the kind offer. He took me into his elevated summer-house.

"I do not reside here, but come occasionally to amuse myself with the prospect (which was fine); have brought a bone of lamb, and wish you to partake."

After a slight apology, I made a hearty dinner, and drank what I chose; in my situation a small draught could not suffice.

From his window, he explained the whole country, attended me on the way, and pointed out every object of use.

"May I, Sir, request the name of the gentleman, who has treated me with the most generous hospitality?"

"The Rev. Michael Wheelwright, of Carlisle."

I now pass a mill, where I was shewn, in a field, the line of the Wall, with the stones hacked up. The field was in tillage. Here the sight is gone for ever.

Pass Drawdikes, the seat of the Aglionby's where many inscriptions have been found.

Before I arrive at Stanwix, and in the road to Tarraby, I pass through a field where Severus's Wall is the identical footway, with his faint ditch by its side.

THE FIFTEENTH STATION

CONGAVALA; NOW STANWIX

DRAWING towards the evening, and this village, I asked an old woman, "if she knew where I could lodge?"

"Yes, I will take you to a house where the people are clean, honest, and civil."

"Upon asking for a bed?

"No; Do *you* think I will turn out my constant customers for you!"

I applied to a second, and received a second "No."

I was directed to a third; saw only the landlady, a fine figure, well dressed, had been a beauty, and *yet* shewed as much of that valuable commodity as could be expected from forty-five.

"Madam, can you favour me with a bed?"

She surveyed me with a small degree of surprize————"No!"

I took a seat.

"I will pay whatever you desire."

"I could spare one; but it will not suit me."

"I have tried to procure one, but am unable. Pray, Madam, indulge me, it is drawing towards nine.--Do not suffer me to lie in the street."

"You are a stranger to me!"

"So I am to every one else. If I must not sleep till I am known, I must walk one hundred and fifty miles for a bed."

"What? are you on foot?"

"Yes; but if I am, I have not the appearance of a common tramper; neither would a horse be of use, except he could mount precipices, and climb over stone walls. Pray, Madam, favour me."

"I am a single woman; and, to take in a stranger, may give rise to reflection."

"Did you ever hear of a woman losing her character by a man of seventy-eight!" (I thought I perceived, pass through her mind, a small ray of pity.)

"I do not keep a public-house."

"I ask pardon, Madam; I applied because I saw a sign over the door."

"It has been a public-house; and the sign was forgot to be taken down."—I retreated.

We met a short time after, when a slight civility passed between us.

A week elapsed, when, dining at a public table in Carlisle, I mentioned this singular adventure. The whole company, in a moment, recognized the person I alluded to, and told me, "She had long been connected with the Duke of———; had issue by him of some standing, who were training for genteel life, whom he allowed her to visit once a year. That whenever he came into those parts, he chose to see her, and that she bore an amiable character." I therefore think she acted perfectly right in refusing admittance.

I afterwards procured a bed, fell a prey to the dancing gentry of the night, and the next morning, turned and shook my shirt, being unwilling to carry off any thing but my own.

The place where this Station was, is easily found; but no marks remain, not even that roughness in the ground which distinguishes every other.

Agricola and Hadrian totally disappear; and all that can be seen of Severus is his ditch, which is nearly obliterated, about two hundred yards long, part of which is a bye lane, and part by the hedge, in the inclosure, fourteen yards wide, and four feet deep: both point to the Station, and down the precipice, fifty feet high, to the river.

I observed a stone in the street, converted into a horse-block, three steps high, with the figure of a man, in a recess, eighteen inches in height, in a Roman dress, and in great preservation. I wonder the boys had not pelted him out of the world. I inquired its history of some elderly people; but all I could learn was, "It stood there before my time." I believe it to be a Roman Chief.

The Wall then proceeds from this elevated Station down the precipice, where it crosses the river Eden, to Carlisle; and makes a remarkable bend to the right, evidently to cross at the narrowest part, and to include the city, which was a place of consequence in the time of the Britons. There are but two places of magnitude in the whole line of the Wall, Newcastle, and Carlisle, and it makes a turn to grasp in both.

Stanwix is but about four hundred yards East of this city; and that space consists of meadow and water; perhaps, in a flood, all water.

The Wall points very near the North foot of the Castle-hill, keeping the Eden on the right, all the way to the sea.

While in the desolate, the rocky, the mountainous regions, I enjoyed the pleasing curiosities of the Wall, the banks, the Stations, &c.; but, now I am travelling in the beautiful and cultivated parts, I am travelling without my friends. I search, but cannot find them.

Camden, and Warburton, "thought the river formerly ran near the Castle, at Carlisle, and had changed its course since the time of the Romans;" but give no reason. From a survey of the ground, I think it has not.

At Kirkandrews, I saw a precipice, along which the Wall had run, and where it did not need a trench. One hundred yards within the Wall, I saw, running through a corn-field, the faint remains of Agricola's and Hadrian's works. Some little may also be seen near Wormanby, and at Beaumont.

THE SIXTEENTH STATION

AXELODUNUM; NOW BURGH

ALTHOUGH Severus, wherever he could, chose high ground for his Station, and his Wall; yet here he was obliged to chuse, for the first, a low meadow, about two hundred yards East of the church, called *The Old Castle;* the foundations of which are visible; the whole about the usual size, one hundred and thirty-six yards square. I am now five miles West of Carlisle, and eight from Boulness.

I was taken into a garden where a stone with a Roman inscription was shewn me; but none of us could read it.

In the belfry of the church, they shewed me a door about five feet high, but very wide, made of iron bars, resembling a jail window, once a prison door of the Castle.

I overtook a farmer driving his team. "Sir," says he, "are you a Doctor?" (a Quack, no doubt, with my budget stuffed with laxatives.)

"No, I am not; but I can prescribe at a venture, as the Faculty often do. What question do you wish to have solved?"

"I have a brother dangerously ill."

"What is his complaint?"

"We cannot tell; but he has kept his bed eighteen weeks, and taken nothing but a little wine."

"Then, I fear, your brother is not long for this world."

How easily I might have picked up a fee! I was sorry for him. He felt for a brother!

Stones have been frequently ploughed up at Burgh with the mortar adhering to them, which shews the annihilated state of the Wall; nay, I believe every farmer, through the whole line from sea to sea, can point out the spot where it ran in his own ground.

Edward the First, resolving to reduce Scotland, assembled an army, and encamped upon the sands, a mile from the town, on my right; but was seized with a flux, and carried off. Upon the spot of his departure, Henry Howard, Duke of Norfolk, proprietor of the land, erected a monument, twenty-eight feet high, in 1685, declaring the event, in Latin.

Time and the weather, have reduced this monument; and the fragments now lie round the spot. Lord Londsale is proprietor of the estate, by exchange of property with the Duke, and, I was informed, had promised to erect another; which the country wait for, or would erect it themselves. Edward's bowels are said to have been interred in the church.

After quitting Burgh, which is a long, flat place, and deemed the largest village in Cumberland, we enter a flat marsh, three or four miles square, the road in the centre; the marsh is sometimes overflowed with the sea, is full of cattle, and deep ditches, to carry off the tide. I cannot suppose, that either the Wall or the mounds ran along this marsh.

As Severus certainly proceeded on our right through Burgh, and as certainly crosses the road from left to right, as we rise the hill, at the extremity of the marsh, entering Dramburgh; it proves that the Wall crossed the way at Burgh, and proceeded a considerable way on our left, out of the reach of both marsh and tide.

Jaded with labour, nature calling for sustenance, and melted with a July sun, I asked a person, upon this marsh, "what public-house I could apply to at Drumburgh?"

"There is none," he replied.

"Then, like other beggars, I must try the Christian charity of some kind inhabitant; for there is no supporting life without food, and rest; and money itself is of no use, when the thing we want cannot be purchased."

He offered me his horse, and gave me a pressing invitation to his house; but it lay too wide.

I entered the Castle, made a slight apology to a woman engaged at the fire, in dishabille, whom I supposed was the mistress, and the only person there.—I sat down.—She returned no answer.—I held a momentary conversation by way of filling up the time, and winning the stake in view. She not only refused a reply, but would not even look at me.—I considered myself an unwelcome guest, and entertained the idea of departing.—She retreated without either word or look, and I gave up all for lost.

In two or three minutes she returned in a better dress, loosely put on, with a large tumbler of brandy and water. Former shyness was dissipated in a moment; Female delicacy, I perceived, had been wounded, by what she thought an unbecoming dress, exposed to the eye of a stranger.

The whole family instantly became friendly with me. I was pressed to dinner, to spend the day, and to take a bed; all which I declined; for I considered *time* the most valuable article I possessed.

THE SEVENTEENTH STATION

GABROSENTUM; NOW DRUMBURGH

I AM Now nine miles from Carlisle, and four from Boulness, the termination of the Wall. The Castle stands upon a rising ground, at the extremity of the marsh; and was erected by the Dacres, two hundred years ago, with the materials of the old Castle, and upon the old foundation. Their arms are placed in the front. It is no more than a large, handsome farm-house.

My kind friend took me, with a candle, into the lower regions; where I saw "darkness visible," which brought to mind the horrors of a dungeon.

Though the dim light could not carry the eye to the extremity of the thickness of the Wall, yet I could perceive it was three or four yards thick, and seemed to be formed for eternity.

The site of the Station, now an orchard, garden, &c. is, with the ramparts, perfectly plain. My friend too, directed my eye to the course of Severus's Wall, which came from the South of the marsh, crossed the turnpike road at the Station, and would proceed on my right, where I perceived Severus's trench fourteen yards wide, and four feet deep.

At the bottom of the land, three miles farther, where I open to the sea, the wall crosses the road, and continues to run one hundred yards on my left. Here I saw the Wall recently stocked up, and the stones laid on heaps for future use.

At this lane's end, the noble works of Agricola and Hadrian are supposed to have terminated; which is probable.

One mile prior to the extremity of our journey, and at the distance of one inclosure on our left, appears in majesty, for the last time, Severus's Wall, being five or six hundred yards long, and three feet high; but, as in the mountains, all confusion. A fence grows upon it, which becomes its security from an arrest either by time, or the wicked hands of man. In two places it is six feet high, eight broad, and three thick; but has no facing-stones.

The cruel farmer gloried, "that his sacrilegious fingers had destroyed such and such a part of the Wall."

"I hoped," in reply, "the next stone he disturbed might break his mattock; and begged not one of them might be touched *till my return*."

He made a promise to my wish, perhaps as binding as that of a lover.

I saw *Gretna Green,* that source of repentance; but, being myself half a century above par, and not having with me an amorous lass of eighteen with as many thousands, I had no occasion for the black-smith.

My landlord and his wife, where I slept at S———, had been handsome. She told me, "that hers was a Gretna Green wedding, which cost a few guineas; and that she was descended from a good family." But it was easy to see, that poverty, a pot of ale, and the sorrow of fifteen years, were the result.

The Rev. John P———, however, does not always act the farce for a few guineas. Interest prompts him to carry a stamp of every dimension; and he sometimes procures a note of a hundred from the happy bridegroom, which stands a chance for payment should the lady's papa come to a reconciliation.

THE EIGHTEENTH STATION

TUNNOCELUM; NOW BOULNESS

NOTHING is left of this Station but the spot which marks it, upon a rock on the verge of Solway Frith, thirteen miles West of Carlisle.

Severus must have done almost infinite service to the world, by erecting the Wall. Half the churches, houses, barns, partition-walls, and roads, nay, even down to a very horse-block, were raised out of this Wall. Here the church and village of Boulness had their origin.

Whether the extremity of the Station was made perfectly secure, by carrying it far enough into the water, is doubtful; for the Scots frequently came over the Frith, at low tide, in bodies; murdered, burnt, carried off their booty; and drove away their cattle.

In 1216, they stayed rather too long before their return, owing to a thirst of gain; when their whole body, with all the property, was swept away by the tide.

Our historians say, "The river was choaked up with the multitude." They never saw the extent of the Frith, or they would not have ventured the expression.

Horses, carts, &c. frequently pass over at low water. As I walked by these sands to Boulness, they seemed dry, a small gutter or two excepted.

Weary, and melted, I dined at a public-house; but was surprized when I returned, three hours after, to see a vast expanse of sea at my feet, with vessels of magnitude sailing upon its surface.

Scotland, on the opposite shore, looked beautiful.

I now approach Carlisle, where I first entered, having crossed the kingdom twice, under a burning sun, and, without a drop of rain, in seven days and six hours.

CONCLUSION

HAVING thus far proceeded in my laborious, my romantic, and even my Quixotic undertaking, the double tour of the Wall; I shall close the work with some remarks upon the Authors who have gone before me; upon the mode of building the Wall, and the nature of the stone. I shall give a concise list of the Stations and the intermediate places, from the East to the West end of this grand line. I shall notice the inscriptions; state my return, and the journal of the day.

I am more confirmed in my opinion, that none of the writers ever passed the whole length of the Wall; that very few have ever seen it; but that the first Historian, however ignorant, like the first horse in a team, was implicitly followed by the rest.

An old Author says, "Hadrian was the *first* who drew a rampart of prodigious bulk, as high as a *mountain!*" This proves he never saw it, nor knew its history.

Another evidently mistakes Antoninus's work in Scotland, for Severus's in England.

A third says, "The Wall was begun by *Hadrian,* and finished by Severus." This supposes only one work.

A fourth says, "Severus only *repaired* Hadrian's Wall.

A fifth, "The Wall was thirty-five miles long."

A sixth, "One hundred and twenty-two miles long."

Even the venerable *Bede* "cannot allow that Severus built a Wall, because *Wall* implies a work of stone. Can we suppose, that he ever saw, thought, or inquired about it? although a neighbour to the place. He, and Gildas, both observe, "that, when the Romans quitted the Island, they advised the *Britons* to build a Wall from sea to sea, to keep out the enemy;" which shews how little they knew of the matter. Yet these are reputed our best antient writers.

Again. "They made the Wall between two straits, or bays of the sea, a thousand miles!" Surely this must be charged to the printer.

Some authors have amused themselves and readers with a brass pipe running through the internal part of the Wall, to convey intelligence.

From the above absurdities, and fifty more which I could select, can a reader form a regular set of ideas, as he peruses a work? The eye of the Historian should see; and it rests with him to cause the reader to see as he does.

From the destruction of so large a part of these magnificent works, I fear, I shall be the last Author who shall describe them. Plunder is the order of the day. I wished to see Severus's works in a superior style, but am an age too late. They have suffered more during the last century, than in the fifteen before.

THE BUILDING

SOME authors say, "Hadrian's *Wall,*" *as they term it,* "*is built of earth and stone:*" *but I believe there was no more stone than was promiscuously thrown out, with the soil of the neighbouring ditch, of which it is composed.*

Again: "that Severus's Wall is faced with casing-stones on the outside, and the internal part filled up with stones placed in an oblique direction." Part of this remark is true. The stones are faced on both sides of the Wall, and very often shaped in a diagonal line, that is, like the key stone of an arch, and always laid with the end to the front, although three or four feet long, the narrow and broad end alternately, by way of dove-tail; and the internal part *not laid at all,* but stones of all sizes promiscuously thrown in, and the mortar as promiscuously thrown in among them.

I tried the strength of the mortar, and found it equal to that of stone.

STONE

I SHALL find it difficult to support an opinion when all the world, from Bede to the present day, are against me; to which must be added that of the whole country. But, as it is not the fashion, as in a former day, to burn a man for his opinion, allow me to state mine, and I will attend to yours.

All agree, "that the stone of which Severus's Wall was built is not a native of the country, for the grit differs."—But no evidence is produced where it *was* brought from.

I observed only two kinds of stone in the whole line; and with both, the country abounds. That towards the East has a whitish covering, like unbleached linen, is a flinty texture, and when broken is nearly the colour of lead.

That towards the West is of a softer nature, brown, a little the colour of saffron. Of this the cathedral and walls of Carlisle are composed; and the Wall of Severus seems to have been made of these. They seem, also, to be the same kind as those I saw stocked up at St. Oswald's, at Hare-hill, and at Boulness. I observed too, several places where stone had been got. Besides, it is not easy to see how they could bring from a distance so vast a load; neither the reason, when there was abundance which suited at home. Perhaps this is one of those wonders which takes possession of the human mind, ever fond of, and ever seeking after the wonderful.

INSCRIPTIONS

I HAVE treated but little of Roman inscriptions, or of Legions, and Cohorts, for several reasons. They are all totally vanished from the Wall and Stations where they were placed. Some few have been preserved by the connoisseur, in dusty lumber-rooms, which seldom see light; more are converted into slabs, steps, lintels, or used for viler purposes; and still more are destroyed.

The few inscriptions that remain are nearly obliterated; and, where they not, they are written in half characters, and in Latin, not easy to understand; and, being unacquainted with the Latin tongue, it might seem presumption in me to attempt it. Besides, with what success could I explain that, about which the Learned themselves differ? And, if they could be explained, what do they amount to? only that such a regiment, or company, resided in a certain place, when all are equally unknown; and to the generality of readers, nothing is more dry. When he has laboured through a parcel of miserable letters, what is he the wiser?

I allow, a stone of such antiquity becomes a curiosity; but a piece of antiquity, when not understood, sinks in value; and still more, if not of moment. The hungry inquirer, who can relish a dry husk, may find in Warburton all which have been discovered in latter ages, to the number of one hundred and fifty-two; also in my friend Mr. Gough's edition of Camden's Britannia.

I design this work a present to a Bookseller. As it will be cheap to him, I wish it cheap to the purchaser. I would have it sweet as the apple; but, if I load it with parings, like putting garlick into his repast, it will swell the book, the price, and the disgust.

I SHALL concisely state, from the Wall's end to Boulness, every Station as it occurs; with the intermediate places through or by which this grandest of all British monuments passed.

1. WALL'S END.—By Cousen's house, now Baddle's—Slate's house—Stile in the Valley—Old Walker's-hill—Byker's hill—A windmill—Crosses the road thirty yards North of the Toll-gate—Eswburn—Redburns—Another windmill—Pandon Gate.

2. NEWCASTLE—Near the West gate—On the right towards the Toll gate—Crosses the road, and runs twenty yards left of the Quarry house—Elswick

windmill—Fenham Lodge—Mr. Orde's house—Mr. Bowes's house.

3. BENWELL HILL—Mr. Orde's other house—Denton Dean—Chapel houses—Mr. Mountague's house on the left—Wallbottle—Newburn Dean—Throcklow.

4. RUTCHESTER—High Seat—Harlow hill—Wall houses—Sir Edward Blacket's—Halton Shields.

5. HALTON CHESTERS—Port Gate—St. Oswald—North Tyne river.

6. WALWICK CHESTERS, or East Chesters—Walwick—Towertay.

7. CARROWBURGH—Carrow—Shewenshields—Ethel's Chair—Cat's Cover—Busy Gap.

8. HOUSE STEADS—Haltwhistle Burn.

9. LITTLE CHESTERS—Wall Green.

10. GREAT CHESTERS—Cock-Mount-Hill—Wall Town—Wintergap Cross.

11. CARVORAN—Tippal river—Thirlwell Castle—Stone Gap—Willoford—Poltross—Irthing.

12. BURDOSWALD—Midgham foot—Wallbowers—The Banks—Hare Hill—Bank Head—Birchshaw—Randilands—High-Wall-Town.

13. CAMBECK FORT, or rather House Steads—Irthington—Newton—Comeranton—Old-Wall-Town—Wall Head.

14. WATCH CROSS—Bleatern—Wallby—Taraby.

15. STANWIX—Cross the Eden—North of Carlisle Castle—Kirkandrews—Beaumont.

16. BURGH—On the right a windmill—South of the Marsh.

17. DRUMBURGH—Glaston—Kirklands.

18. BOULNESS.

RETURN

I NOW quit the favourite Wall, perhaps for ever; where I entered a stranger, and returned well known: for many knew me who had never before seen me; they had heard of the man in black, with his green umbrella and black pouch; and I have reason to think, from the treatment I met with, I could travel the Wall a third time, with the expence only of a few shillings.

I quitted it at Carlisle, where I first entered, after crossing the kingdom twice, between the German ocean and the Irish sea.

In the evening, after walking twenty-eight miles, I approached Hesket, ten miles South of Carlisle, and seeing two or three signs before me, I asked a person "which of them could furnish me with the best lodging?" "There is none that will suit you. Go to the upper village;" where I succeeded.

The next day I passed through Penrith, Clifton, Lord Lonsdale's grounds, which are not so beautiful as they might easily be made, and stopping at the next village to dine, the name I think is Thrimby, I found the larder thinly stored. There was no meat, porter, cyder, or liquors; and, as I could not drink ale, I gladly accepted a dish of milk.

A landlady is not apt to smile upon the man who is unfriendly to the tap. I remarked, "A thunder-storm is coming on? I will stay a little longer." She replied, "You may get to *Shap* (four miles) before it comes. Besides, there is a farm-house, two miles off, where you may shelter." This was a hint to depart. I paid sixpence. She was giving me change. I told her "to keep the groat,"—she smiled; and I *might* have staid longer.

Before I arrived at the two-mile house I was caught in the storm. I entered the fold-yard, with a view to secure myself in one of the out-buildings. "I will beg leave, madam, to shelter a little while."

"The storm," says she, "is over," casting an eye upwards.

This was a second hint to depart, which I obeyed. A terrible rain ensued.

I was directed to a public-house in Shap, I think the *Hound,* "where I should be well accommodated;" but, when I arrived, I found about half the building was taking down for repairs. They treated me kindly, and promised a bed; but, when the hour of rest came, I was taken through the rain to a neighbour's, where they had provided one for me. I found it was upon a solid ground floor, where every think felt cold about me; the bed perfectly damp. I was obliged to rise, half dress, and lie between the blankets.

I left a shilling upon the table, and retreated at four the next morning, without seeing one soul; nor do I know whether the house was inhabited.

SHAP FELLS

I IMMEDIATELY entered upon these Fells, a region which surprized me. During six miles did I wander over a most barren and solitary desert, without the sight of a human being, a house, cottage, tree, or even an acre of cultivated ground. The freehold could not be worth half a crown an acre. Had the proprietor been there, he would have blushed to own the property. Had George the Third been there, he would have been sorry he was King over such a region.

All the prospect before me was only hills upon hills; and yet this could not be the place to which *David* referred, when he said, from the ALMIGHTY, "The cattle upon a thousand hills are mine;" for, although there *are* a thousand hills, yet all the cattle I saw upon them were not worth fifty pounds. It was more probably the place were *Jove* and the *Giants* fought, and where they pelted him with mountains; for there was ammunition enough.

My road led me through Kendal, a large, handsome, populous town, and in a fertile country. The castle stands in a beautiful spot; but is, like others, in ruins.

Slept at Burton, twenty miles; and the next morning breakfasted with my little family, at *Hest Bank*, nine miles.

We stayed in this delightful place four days; and were still more delighted with the company we found there. If to enjoy social conversation with freedom, and with sensible people; if fascinating mirth attending the hours as they pass, and friendship rising to the highest pitch to which it can rise in so short a period,—constitute happiness; I must rate these four days among the happiest of my life. These agreeable associates were from Kirkby Lonsdale. I am sorry delicacy hides their names.

By easy marches I arrived at Birmingham, August 7, 1801; after a loss, by perspiration, of one stone of animal weight; an expenditure of forty guineas; a lapse of thirty-five days; and a walk of six hundred and one miles.

As so long and solitary a journey on foot was, perhaps, never wantonly performed by a man of seventy-eight, it has excited the curiosity of the town; and causes me frequently to be stopped in the street to ascertain the fact. I shall, "to satisfy all whom it may concern," give the Journal of the day, in the following table.

THE JOURNAL

1801.			Slept at	Miles.	Addit.	Total.
July	4,	Sat.	Lichfield			16
	5,	Sun.	Stone			22
	6,	M.	Hulmes Chapel			25
	7,	Tu.	Warrington	18	1	19
	8,	W.	Liverpool	18	3	21
	9,	Th.	Ditto.			
	10,	F.	Tarlton			21
	11,	Sat.	Garstang			21
	12,	Sun.	Haysham	17	3	20
	13,	M.	Ditto			
	14,	Tu.	Hest Bank			6
	15,	W.	Newby Bridge	18	1	19
	16,	Th.	Ambleside	15	1	16
	17,	F.	Penrith			25
	18,	Sat.	Stanwix	20	1	21
	19,	Sun.	Burgh (return from Boulness)			22
	20,	M.	High Walton			15
	21,	Tu.	Twice Brewed			14
	22,	W.	Harlow Hill			22
	23,	Th.	Newcastle	17	1 return	18
	24,	F.	Walwick Chesters			22
	25,	Sat.	Glyn Velt			18
	26,	Sun.	Hesket			28
	27,	M.	Shap			19
	28,	Tu.	Burton			20

Date	Day	Place			
29,	W.	Hest Bank			9
30,	Th.	Ditto			
31,	F.	Ditto		3	3
Aug. 1,	Sat.	Ditto			
2,	Sun.	Preston	25	1	26
3,	M.	Wigan			17
4,	Tu.	Knutsford			25
5,	W.	Newcastle under Line			24
6,	Th.	Wolsley Bridge			21
7,	F.	Saltley, near Birmingham			26
					601